The STORY of the WORLD'S Greatest PAINTINGS

THE ARNOLFINI PORTRAIT   THE BATTLE OF SAN ROMANO
PRIMAVERA   MONA LISA   CHILDREN'S GAMES   AN OLD WOMAN
COOKING EGGS   THE ART OF PAINTING   THE SKATE   SELF-
PORTRAIT HESITATING BETWEEN THE ARTS OF MUSIC AND
PAINTING   THE MONK BY THE SEA   THE RAFT OF THE MEDUSA
THE HAY WAIN   A BURIAL AT ORNANS   OPHELIA   LA LOGE
BREEZING UP (A FAIR WIND)   SUMMER'S DAY   A SUNDAY ON LA
GRANDE JATTE   MONT SAINTE-VICTOIRE   WHERE DO WE COME
FROM? WHAT ARE WE? WHERE ARE WE GOING?

 Thames & Hudson

Charlie Ayres

This book is dedicated to Saskia,
an artist in the making

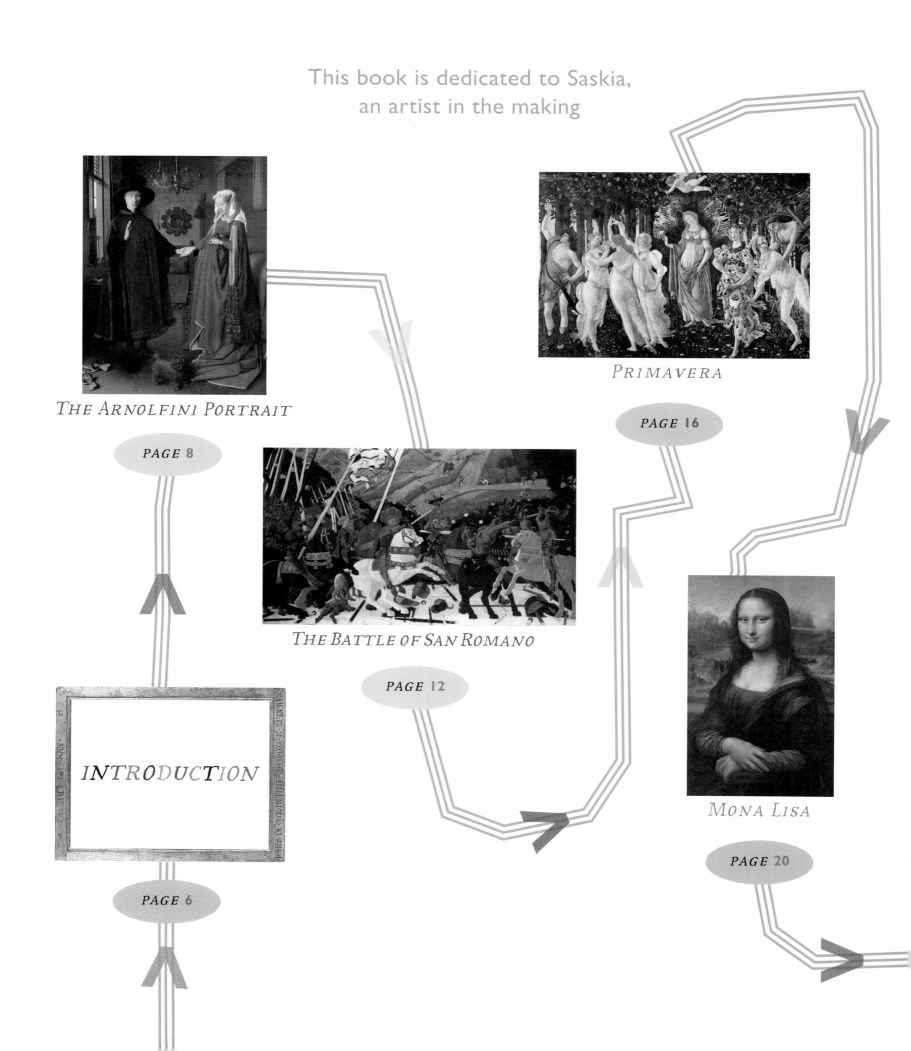

THE ARNOLFINI PORTRAIT

PRIMAVERA

THE BATTLE OF SAN ROMANO

MONA LISA

INTRODUCTION

The STORY of the WORLD'S Greatest PAINTINGS

CHILDREN'S GAMES

PAGE 24

AN OLD WOMAN COOKING EGGS

PAGE 28

THE ART OF PAINTING

PAGE 32

THE SKATE

PAGE 36

SELF-PORTRAIT HESITATING
BETWEEN THE ARTS OF
MUSIC AND PAINTING

PAGE 40

SUMMER'S DAY

PAGE 72

BREEZING UP (A FAIR WIND)

PAGE 68

LA LOGE

PAGE 64

A SUNDAY ON
LA GRANDE JATTE

PAGE 76

MONT SAINTE-VICTOIRE

PAGE 80

WHERE DO WE COME FROM?
WHAT ARE WE? WHERE ARE WE GOING?

PAGE 84

THE MONK BY THE SEA

THE RAFT OF THE MEDUSA

THE HAY WAIN

OPHELIA

A BURIAL AT ORNANS

Chronologies of the Artists

Museums to Visit

Glossary

Picture Credits

INTRODUCTION

WHY do people want to become artists? Why do they choose to paint, and what do they hope to achieve when they first pick up a brush? For thousands of years, men and women have painted pictures of real and imaginary worlds. They have painted stories and still lifes, people and landscapes, vast historical scenes and small intricate interiors. They have made their living from painting pictures and occasionally – just occasionally – they have created masterpieces.

This book takes as its subject twenty such masterpieces, ranging in date from the fifteenth to the nineteenth century, and looks at how each was created, who it was made for and what people have thought of it over the years. Some of these paintings are world famous today, but were little known when they were painted. Others – such as Théodore Géricault's THE RAFT OF THE MEDUSA – were seen as sensational from the moment they were painted.

By travelling back in time we can look at each great work of art as it is being painted. We can creep up on Paul Cézanne and watch him as he paints MONT SAINTE-VICTOIRE, a mountain near his childhood home, which he studies and sketches obsessively. And we can see John Everett Millais make poor Elizabeth Siddal, who posed for his painting OPHELIA, lie in a bath for so long that she catches a horrible cold!

Some artists chose to tell stories in their paintings. Sandro Botticelli's PRIMAVERA is based on an ancient Roman myth about the arrival of spring, while in SELF-PORTRAIT HESITATING BETWEEN THE ARTS OF MUSIC AND PAINTING, Angelica Kauffman painted the moment she decided on her future career. Other artists took famous episodes from history, as Paolo Uccello did with his BATTLE OF SAN ROMANO. Some paintings ask big questions of both the artist and the viewer. Caspar David Friedrich's THE MONK BY THE SEA raises questions about our place in the world, while Paul Gauguin found that creating his epic WHERE DO WE COME FROM? WHAT ARE WE? WHERE ARE WE GOING? exhausted him both physically and mentally.

Other artists chose to represent aspects of the world they saw around them. Pieter Bruegel's *CHILDREN'S GAMES* is a riot of activity, featuring hundreds of children playing a variety of games from bowls to blind man's buff. Gustave Courbet took a more sombre subject for *A BURIAL AT ORNANS*, but presented this everyday scene on a huge scale, rivalling traditional history paintings. Georges Seurat also chose to represent a scene from the world around him in *A SUNDAY ON LA GRANDE JATTE*. All these artists challenged what was considered to be the best style or subject for painting during their lifetimes, and created masterpieces in the process.

We can also see how painting techniques changed over time. Jan van Eyck's *THE ARNOLFINI PORTRAIT* is so detailed it is impossible to see his brushstrokes. Berthe Morisot's *SUMMER'S DAY*, by contrast, is covered in rapid zigzag movements, broad brushstrokes that some critics thought made her work look sketchy and impressionistic, but others saw as capturing the ever-changing world perfectly.

By looking at great works of art we can enter the worlds these artists lived in. We can glimpse the room Johannes Vermeer used as his studio in *THE ART OF PAINTING* and sit on the quayside with Winslow Homer as he makes his preliminary sketches for *BREEZING UP (A FAIR WIND)*. We can follow Constable to his childhood haunts in *THE HAY WAIN*, and watch two models pose as a fashionable Parisian couple at the opera in Pierre-Auguste Renoir's *LA LOGE*. We can see Diego Velázquez positioning his servants in a gloomy kitchen for *AN OLD WOMAN COOKING EGGS*, and smell the fish Jean-Baptiste-Siméon Chardin arranged for his still life *THE SKATE.*

But what is probably the most famous painting in the world refuses to tell us very much about itself. Sitting behind bullet-proof glass in the Louvre Museum in Paris, Leonardo da Vinci's *MONA LISA* smiles at us. She sits in front of an invented landscape on a high balcony, with her hands resting on the arm of a chair. Leonardo kept the painting with him until he died, and it only came to be celebrated as a masterpiece long after his death. Now this small unassuming portrait is famous for being famous, and each year five million people visit the Louvre just to see it. You can study a reproduction of it in this book and maybe go and visit it yourself. Or you may choose to visit one of the other masterpieces. Every one has a fascinating story of its own to tell you.

Charlie Ayres

THE ARNOLFINI PORTRAIT
Jan van Eyck

Jan van Eyck (c. 1390–1441) is famous for using slow-drying oil paints to create finely detailed paintings. *The Arnolfini Portrait* is one of his best-known works, and shows the Italian merchant Giovanni Arnolfini and his wife surrounded by objects that tell us about their life.

This painting used to be called *The Arnolfini Marriage* because it was thought to show the couple's wedding. Some experts still believe the pose of the man and woman and Van Eyck's signature on the back wall (as if he were a witness) suggest this. What do you think? People also used to think the lady was pregnant, but this style of dress was just the fashion at the time.

1434

It is a mild spring day as Jan van Eyck enters Giovanni di Nicolao Arnolfini's house in the Flemish city of Bruges. He is shown upstairs by a servant, and asked to wait in the reception room. The shutters are open, and he can smell cherry blossom. He gently puts down the parcel he is carrying on the wooden chest by the window. At that moment, Arnolfini enters. He is a slender man, with pale skin, pronounced eyes and a long nose. Van Eyck notices how his ears lie flat against his head. Arnolfini has been outside, and takes off his black straw hat and shoes as he says hello.

Arnolfini has invited Van Eyck to his new house because he wants him to paint a portrait of himself and his wife standing in this room. He asks Van Eyck about his reputation for painting things realistically. By way of an answer, Van Eyck picks up the parcel he has brought. He carefully unwraps it and passes Arnolfini a small portrait of a man wearing a red headdress. Arnolfini looks at it for a moment, then glances up at Van Eyck. It is a self-portrait, and Arnolfini is impressed. Van Eyck hasn't made himself look more handsome than he is, but instead has carefully copied the wrinkles around his bloodshot eyes and the stubble on his chin. Arnolfini admires this — it is a true likeness.

✳ look at this

This convex mirror is shaped like a dome to reflect the whole room. In it, beyond the Arnolfini couple, we can see two people standing in the doorway. One of them may be the artist, the other might represent you, the viewer. Above the mirror an inscription appears as if written on the wall like graffiti. It reads: Johannes de eyck fuit hic (Jan van Eyck was here) 1434.

✳ look at this

Many of the objects in *The Arnolfini Portrait* are symbols meant to suggest things to the viewer. The oranges are one example. They were expensive and tell us that Arnolfini was rich. Another example is this little dog, who is here to tell us that the man and woman are faithful to one another. Van Eyck used strokes of many different colours to paint the dog.

DID YOU KNOW?

✳ Beds were found in most rooms in houses like Arnolfini's. This room is where he would talk to visitors, rather than sleep.

✳ Van Eyck often signed and dated his pictures on the frames.

✳ He became court painter to the Duke of Burgundy and was often sent abroad on diplomatic missions.

*Presumed self-portrait
by Jan van Eyck, aged 43*

Van Eyck asks if Arnolfini has any thoughts about what he and his wife want to wear for the portrait. Arnolfini has made a lot of money selling expensive silks and fabrics, and he is always well-dressed. He opens the chest by the window and pulls out a bolt of grass-green fabric. He tells Van Eyck he is going to have it made into a dress for his wife to wear in the portrait. It will be lined with ermine fur and elaborately stitched. He jokes it will probably take as long to sew as the portrait will take to complete.

Van Eyck just smiles. He knows the portrait will take a very long time. First he has to buy an oak panel and cover it with a smooth layer of plaster called 'gesso'. This will provide him with a white surface or 'ground' on which to work. To make the paint, he will grind different pigments and mix them with linseed oil to form coloured pastes. After sketching the figures and the room on to the white ground, he will use the pastes to block in the main colours – green for the new dress, red for the bed covers.

Oil paints dry slowly, and Van Eyck will have to wait for more than a week before he can start building up each section of the painting with layers of thin glazes. He will bring the scene to life

✳ compare this

Painted a year after *The Arnolfini Portrait*, this painting shows Nicolas Rolin, Chancellor of the Duchy of Burgundy, praying in front of the Madonna and Child. Look at the veins standing out on Rolin's head and his cauliflower ear. Van Eyck didn't flatter his sitters, did he? He wanted to paint everything in a realistic way and included lots of details: look for the magpies and peacocks on the balcony.

WHY DON'T YOU?

Experiment with reflections. Objects reflected in the centre of a convex surface like the back of a spoon appear big, while things around the edges seem smaller. Turn the spoon over and the opposite is true of the concave surface inside.

* Compare this

This huge altarpiece, painted by Van Eyck and his brother Hubert, was finished two years before *The Arnolfini Portrait* was painted. Van Eyck took over when Hubert died in 1426. Look at the way he painted the folds of material on the central figures, particularly John the Baptist's green cloak. As with the green dress in the Arnolfini painting — parts of which he blended with his thumb — Van Eyck took great care to make the folds seem real.

● ● ● ● ● ● ● ● ● ● ● ● ● ● ● ● ● ● ● ●

WANT TO SEE MORE?

www.jan-van-eyck.org
www.abcgallery.com/E/eyck/eyck.html
www.nationalgallery.org.uk/paintings/
jan-van-eyck-the-arnolfini-portrait

by painting the way the light from the window illuminates the room, adding shadows to the folds of fabric and highlights to the brass chandelier. He will ensure that each object appears as it does in real life, painting in the grain of the floorboards and the reflection in the expensive convex mirror.

Van Eyck asks his patron if there is anything else he wants included in the portrait. Arnolfini's family comes from Lucca in Italy and he asks Van Eyck to include Italian oranges somewhere. Oranges are a great luxury in Bruges and they will remind Arnolfini of his roots, as well as demonstrate how successful he has become. He also shows Van Eyck a patterned Middle Eastern carpet he has recently bought, and asks if that can be included. Van Eyck agrees, and says goodbye. He heads down the stairs and back home. It is time to start work.

THE BATTLE OF SAN ROMANO
Paolo Uccello

Paolo Uccello (c. 1397–1475) was one of the leading artists of his generation. Many of his paintings were frescoes and are now lost or badly damaged, but fortunately his three paintings of the battle of San Romano have survived. They now hang in three different locations, but were originally commissioned to hang together.

This painting is one of three panels commemorating the Florentine victory over the neighbouring city of Siena in 1432. Uccello has made them very decorative, with swirling banners, gold lances and silver armour, not unlike expensive medieval tapestries. But he has also used the newly discovered technique of perspective to give his paintings depth and bring them to life. Look at the broken lances and the man in armour on the ground in this panel – together they form a grid pattern that gets smaller as it recedes into the distance.

DID YOU KNOW?

✳ Uccello wasn't the painter's real surname – he was called Paolo di Dono – but he so liked painting birds that his friends called him Paolo Uccelli – 'Paul of the Birds' – and the name stuck.

✳ Once Uccello was painting a fresco for a monastery where the abbot only gave him cheese pie and cheese soup to eat. Uccello ran away and wouldn't come back until the abbot promised to feed him properly!

✳ Uccello named his first son Donato after his best friend, the artist Donatello.

1440

The sun has just risen, but Paolo Uccello has already left his house in Florence, Italy, and is walking to his workshop. He wants to get there early so he can make sure his three paintings of the battle of San Romano are finished before his patrons, the Bartolini Salimbeni family, ask to see them.

Uccello squints in the morning sun as he walks through the square in front of Santa Maria Novella, a church where he painted two frescoes eight years ago. He heads towards his workshop, which is opposite the baptistery of Florence's cathedral. Uccello knows the area well. At the age of ten, he had joined the studio of the sculptor Lorenzo Ghiberti and spent eight years of his life working there while Ghiberti was making the baptistery's huge bronze doors. The sculptor Donatello, still Uccello's best friend, had also been one of Ghiberti's assistants.

Donatello is one of the first artists to have understood the idea of perspective, and he uses it to make his relief sculptures seem more believable. Uccello wants to do the same in his paintings. Based on mathematics, perspective is a technique that allows artists to trick viewers into thinking they are actually looking at a real scene. It makes things that are supposed to be far away appear smaller. Uccello loves experimenting with perspective, using it to make objects seem three-dimensional. In some of his works he uses it to add drama, but he also uses it decoratively, to make patterns. He has done this in his three paintings of the battle of San Romano.

Portrait of Paolo Uccello, with his fellow artists Giotto on the left and Donatello on the right

✳ look at this

During the battle, the leader of the Florentine army Niccolò da Tolentino held off an attack by a much bigger Sienese army for eight hours. Instead of painting Tolentino in battle dress, Uccello shows him wearing a ceremonial cloak and hat. This allowed Uccello to paint the rich gold and red pattern and to experiment with trying to make the hat look three-dimensional. Do you think he succeeded?

WANT TO SEE MORE?

www.paolouccello.org
www.abcgallery.com/U/uccello/uccello.html
www.nationalgallery.org.uk/paintings/
paolo-uccello-the-battle-of-san-romano

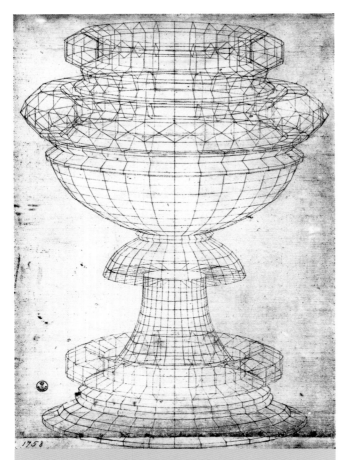

1458

✳ Compare this

Uccello completed many drawings like this one, but only a few have survived. Here he has drawn a chalice, or cup, using geometric shapes to show how it would look in three dimensions. Now look carefully at Niccolò da Tolentino's hat in *The Battle of San Romano*. Uccello probably made a drawing of it first to work out how to make it look three-dimensional. He would lock himself away in his study for days on end, playing around with objects like the chalice and hat, and using perspective to make them seem solid and believable.

WHY DON'T YOU?

Use perspective to draw an avenue of trees. Make a line across a sheet of paper to represent the horizon. Mark a spot at the centre. This is your vanishing point. The outer trees you draw should gradually get smaller and smaller, and closer together, until they reach the vanishing point.

During this famous battle, which took place eight years earlier, the Florentine army defeated troops from the nearby city of Siena. Niccolò da Tolentino was in charge of the army, and Uccello has painted him looking splendid on a white horse in the centre of the first of three wooden panels, his curling white banner flying high above him. The second panel shows the Sienese leader being attacked, and the third shows the victorious Florentine army.

Although Uccello has painted men in armour, they don't really look like they are fighting. Tolentino wears a ceremonial costume, and the men carry long lances normally used for jousting at tournaments. Uccello has painted lots of broken lances on the ground, creating a grid pattern. This pattern shows how perspective works – as they extend back into the picture, the squares of the grid become smaller. The effect is like looking at a tiled floor – the tiles at the back of the room appear smaller than the ones you stand on, even though you know they are all the same size.

Uccello was up late last night drawing, and yawns as he sees the dome of the cathedral ahead. He painted a fresco of another military leader, Sir John Hawkwood, for the cathedral four years ago, but since then they haven't asked him to do anything else. He hopes they will commission him again soon.

He unlocks his workshop and opens the shutters. His paintings appear out of the gloom like giant hunting tapestries, the black and white horses and red and blue harnesses enhanced by the silver armour and the golden lances. Uccello looks at the lances and the patterns they make across the surface of each painting. He loves making patterns. When he was younger, he had spent six years in Venice repairing the sparkling golden mosaics inside the cathedral of San Marco. While there, he had also sketched the horse statues that stood outside the cathedral. Now he is pleased to have brought the two things together in these panels. His paintings of the battle of San Romano gleam with real gold, and feature many horses in different poses. He particularly likes the horses lying on the ground – he has worked for many months trying to get them right, according to the laws of perspective.

Several drawings on a table by the window stir in the breeze and fall to the floor. Uccello picks them up. They are all of horses and birds and are by other artists. Uccello uses them to help him with his paintings. He lays them on the table and looks at his paintings once more. He is pleased with them, and hopes his patrons will be, too.

✳ Compare this

The three panels of Uccello's painting do not join up, but show three separate moments from the battle of San Romano. The panels do, however, balance each other. In the first painting Niccolò da Tolentino sits on a white horse turned to the right. In the third painting, Michelotto da Cotignola, another Florentine leader, sits on a black horse turned to the left. In the middle painting, horses buck, rear, fall and prance. Uccello loved painting horses. How many can you see in the three paintings?

PRIMAVERA
Sandro Botticelli

Sandro Botticelli (1445–1510) was fifteenth-century Florence's greatest painter. He established Greek and Roman mythology as a valid subject for paintings and had many wealthy and important patrons, including the powerful Medici family. *Primavera* is considered his masterpiece.

Primavera illustrates the story of Flora, the goddess of spring, as told in the Roman poet Ovid's book *Fasti*. Flora appears on the right and Venus, the goddess of love, is in the centre. Above her, Cupid shoots an arrow of love towards the Three Graces, who perform a circular dance next to Mercury, the winged messenger of the gods, who is banishing clouds from the garden. The painting was commissioned by Lorenzo di Pierfrancesco de'Medici for his new house, Villa Castello, when he was just nineteen.

1482

It is springtime, and Sandro Botticelli can smell orange blossom. He is standing in his workshop next to his family's house in the Ognissanti quarter of Florence, Italy. It is a relatively poor district of weavers and tanners. Until recently it was the smell of hide being tanned into leather by his father that wafted through the windows. But his father died last year and the tanning equipment now lies idle.

Botticelli could probably afford to move out of the Ognissanti quarter now. He has just returned from working for the Pope in Rome, decorating the walls of the Sistine Chapel. He is a successful painter with a busy studio and three assistants of his own. But he has always lived there with his brothers and doesn't imagine he will ever leave.

He picks up his brush and contemplates the half-painted figures in his latest work, *Primavera* (Springtime). The subject is Flora, the Roman goddess of spring. The painting has been commissioned by Lorenzo di Pierfrancesco de'Medici, a wealthy banker and a member of Florence's most powerful family. Lorenzo is only nineteen but is already a great admirer of ancient philosophers and poets. When he met Botticelli, he recited passages about Flora written by the Roman poet Ovid.

If Botticelli is honest, he is running a bit behind on finishing the painting – it's taken him a while to get on with it. He knows his lack of focus irritates his elder brother Giovanni. Sometimes he doesn't work for days, even though he has many commissions. His assistants dutifully keep painting Madonna and Child pictures that are easy to sell, but sometimes Botticelli himself just doesn't feel like painting. Now, however, he is raring to go.

He looks from left to right across the painting. It is a big wooden panel, two metres high (six and a half feet) and more than three metres wide (ten feet). No one has painted a mythological work of this size, he thinks, since the days of ancient Greece and Rome.

Botticelli has included quite a few figures to tell Flora's story. On the left is Mercury, the messenger of the gods, who is there to get rid of the clouds and protect the garden. Beside him, a group of nymphs known as the Three Graces dance in front of Venus, the goddess of love, who stands in the centre of the painting. Above her head, Venus's

In the fifteenth century, artists mainly made their living painting religious subjects. This painting shows the Bible story of the Three Magi (wise men) bringing gifts to the baby Jesus. The men in the painting seem full of character, but Mary, Jesus's mother, is idealized. Compare her to Venus in *Primavera* — their heads are similarly angled and they wear the same transparent headdress. Even though they are different women, Botticelli has painted them in a similar way. He has also included himself in this painting, looking out. Can you find him?

WANT TO SEE MORE?

www.sandrobotticelli.net
www.historylink101.com/art/
Sandro_Botticelli/bio_Botticelli.htm

blindfolded son Cupid aims his arrow at the nymphs. Next comes Flora, wearing a fashionable dress decorated with flowers. The female figure behind her with flowers coming out of her mouth represents the nymph Chloris, as Flora was known before she married Zephyr, the west wind. Zephyr is shown flying low through the orange trees as he tries to catch her. Flowers grow across the lawn, and the trees bear blossom and fruit at the same time, as if springtime has made everything bloom.

Each time Botticelli works on *Primavera* he has to paint quickly. One of his assistants mixes different coloured pigments with egg yolk to make them into liquid paints, and then he has to blend and apply them to the panel before they dry. He has heard that other artists are starting to experiment with the slower-drying oil paints used in northern Europe, but he doesn't think he will try them. He likes the bright colours he can achieve with tempera, and he doesn't want to change his style.

Self-portrait by
Sandro Botticelli, aged 30

✳ Compare this

This was probably painted to decorate a bed. It shows Venus and Mars, two characters from Roman mythology. Before Botticelli painted *Primavera*, mythological scenes were only used as decoration for furniture. In this painting Venus wears a similar dress to the one she has on in *Primavera*. Although Botticelli idealized the face of the goddess in his paintings, her clothes were modelled on the latest fashions and would have made her appear contemporary. The dress she wears here is a fashionable day dress called a *camicia da giorno*.

DID YOU KNOW?

✳ *Botticelli never got married, saying the very idea gave him nightmares!*

✳ *In 1481 the Pope summoned him to Rome to paint three frescoes for the Sistine Chapel. They are still there, below Michelangelo's famous ceiling.*

✳ *Botticelli loved to play practical jokes on his assistants and would stick paper hats on their paintings of angels when they weren't looking!*

He thinks he will work on Flora's feet today, and is soon carefully painting each toe in turn. He then moves on to her hands, detailing the way her left hand is shaded by her dress full of flowers. He looks at the pattern of hands across the painting. Venus and the younger Flora each raise a hand, as do the dancers, while Mercury holds up his wand. The pattern of hands directs the viewer's eyes across the canvas from right to left, helping the viewer follow Flora's story.

Botticelli looks round and sees his brother Giovanni walking past the window. Giovanni is a large man and he throws a shadow over the panel for a moment. When they were children, Giovanni's nickname was Il Botticello or 'Little Barrel'. Botticelli liked this so much he took it as his own surname. Despite being born Alessandro di Filipepi he has always worked under the name Sandro Botticelli. He realizes his brother hasn't seen him in the workshop, so he decides to creep into the house and make him jump. He loves playing practical jokes on people, and anyway he has had enough of painting for the day.

MONA LISA
Leonardo da Vinci

Leonardo da Vinci (1452–1519) was an architect, engineer, inventor, designer, anatomist and artist. Today he is remembered first and foremost as the painter of the *Mona Lisa*, probably the most famous painting in the world.

Leonardo painted the *Mona Lisa* between 1503 and 1506. A portrait of the noblewoman Lisa del Giocondo, it became known as 'Mona Lisa' because in Italian *mona* is short for *madonna*, which means 'my lady'. Leonardo was so fond of the painting that he never gave it to Lisa's husband, Francesco del Giocondo, who had commissioned it, but kept it with him until he died.

1504

It is a warm May morning and Leonardo da Vinci is sitting on a wooden platform hanging from the ceiling of his studio in Florence, Italy. He is working on a giant drawing – called a 'cartoon' – that he will soon turn into a painting on the wall of the council hall at the Palazzo Vecchio. He has been asked to paint the battle of Anghiari, an historic battle from sixty years earlier, when the Florentine army successfully held off troops from Milan.

Leonardo has been allowed to use the dining hall at the monastery of Santa Maria Novella as a studio. He moved in last autumn with his assistants, and has lived and worked here ever since. Salai and Tommaso, his assistants, have stuck sheets of paper together to make the cartoon the same size as the wall Leonardo has to fill, and they have mounted it with a hanging platform to allow him to work on all of it.

Leonardo isn't able to concentrate today because he can't stop thinking about painting Lisa, the wife of the silk and cloth merchant Francesco del Giocondo. Francesco asked Leonardo to paint his wife's portrait some time ago. Leonardo was short of money and work at the time, and said yes. But since then he has become involved in a large engineering project to change the course of Florence's river, the Arno, and now he has agreed to do the painting at the Palazzo Vecchio. Consequently, he hasn't done much work on the portrait, apart from the landscape background. In part, this is based on his travels around the Arno valley two summers ago. He recently added a bridge that looks like the Ponte Buriano at Arezzo, but he still hasn't begun painting Lisa herself. He bumped into her husband recently, who said he would send Lisa over today so they could start.

Leonardo hears footsteps at the far end of the studio and thinks Lisa is early, but it is just Tommaso, laden down with shopping. He sent him out earlier to pay a few debts at the bank and the barbers, and to pick up some provisions. Tommaso unpacks his purchases, and the two sit down to a lunch of bread, eggs, salad and fruit, with a bottle of wine.

Lisa del Giocondo arrives just as they finish. She is wearing a dark dress with embroidery round the neck. It is a fashionable outfit, in the Spanish style that ladies in Florence like to wear at the moment. Leonardo doesn't care about the latest fashion – men in Florence

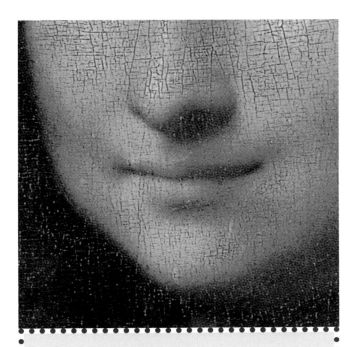

✳ look at this

Leonardo used the style called *sfumato* to paint Lisa's face and her famous smile. He used so many layers of thin glazes that it is impossible to see where one colour blends into another. He used oil paint, a type of paint that was quite new in Italy but had been used for some time in northern Europe by artists such as Jan van Eyck. The slow-drying oil paint allowed him to blend his colours very subtly and he used such fine brushes that you can't see his brushstrokes.

DID YOU KNOW?

✳ Leonardo was fascinated by machinery and designed prototypes of many modern inventions, including planes, helicopters, tanks and bicycles.

✳ To prevent people reading his notebooks, he used back-to-front mirror writing.

✳ Compare this

Lady with an Ermine was painted about fifteen years before the *Mona Lisa* and depicts Cecilia Gallerani, the lover of Ludovico Sforza, the Duke of Milan and one of Leonardo's patrons. Dressed in the latest fashion, she is holding an ermine, an emblem used by the duke after he was awarded an honour known as the Order of the Ermine in 1488. In painting her turning as if looking out of a window, Leonardo uses *contrapposto* to bring her body to life.

currently wear floor-length gowns, but he prefers a knee-length tunic and matching stockings. He is fifty-one years old, and feels it as he looks at the youthful Lisa. She is only twenty-four, and yet has been married for nine years and has three children.

Leonardo explains to Lisa that in the painting it will look as if she's sitting in a loggia, a kind of covered balcony or outdoor room. He positions her near one of the studio windows and studies how the afternoon light falls on her rounded features. He is keen to sketch her pose on to the wooden panel today, and spends time arranging her hands and turning her around in her chair until he is happy.

✳ Compare this

Leonardo kept countless notebooks, and sketched everything from hang-gliders to helicopters, dead bodies to sewage systems. He never tired of drawing people, particularly those who were beautiful, or old and interesting to look at. In this sketch he includes five different studies of heads showing different emotions.

When he is finished, her body is turned sideways, while her face looks straight ahead – a position called *contrapposto*.

Lisa sits for him for a couple of hours before he says she can leave. Leonardo looks at his work so far. He has painted a woman in a similar position before, in *Lady with an Ermine*. He has also included hands in his portraits, and has experimented with capturing smiles. But in this painting of Lisa he is going to bring all these elements together, with a soft touch known as *sfumato*, where the colours are so subtly blended that they look like smoke (*sfumato* actually means 'smoky'). But, for now, he must leave the portrait once more. Lisa will have to be patient.

Portrait of Leonardo da Vinci, attributed to Francesco Melzi, c. 1515–18

WANT TO SEE MORE?

www.da-vinci-gallery.com
www.louvre.fr/llv/dossiers/liste_oal.jsp?bmLocale=en
www.visual-arts-cork.com/old-masters/leonardo-davinci.htm

✳ Compare this

The *Mona Lisa* is not the only one of Leonardo's pictures to show a woman smiling. All the characters in this painting smile, particularly St Anne, who looks down on her daughter, the Virgin Mary, holding baby Jesus. Why do you think Leonardo liked to paint smiles? One theory is that it allowed him to show how good he was at capturing emotions, using his *sfumato* technique. Like the *Mona Lisa*, this painting has a fantastical landscape as its background.

CHILDREN'S GAMES
Pieter Bruegel the Elder

Pieter Bruegel the Elder (1527–1569) was the greatest painter of everyday life in the Netherlands during the sixteenth century. He painted scenes of country weddings, village life and children at play. Although many of his paintings show people having fun, they were also meant to tell stories of right and wrong.

The two hundred children in this painting are all playing games. Some, such as blind man's buff and leapfrog, are still familiar. Others, such as knucklebones, have changed since this picture was painted four and a half centuries ago – now we know the game as 'jacks', and small metal shapes rather than the ankle-bones of sheep are thrown on to the ground! How many games can you spot? Look for the boy on stilts and the children spinning tops.

1560

Pieter Bruegel is watching a play at a dramatic society in the Flemish city of Antwerp. He is with his friend, the engraver Dirck Coornhert. Bruegel makes drawings for the publisher Hieronymus Cock and Coornhert engraves them as prints, which Cock then sells.

Bruegel is enjoying the play. The actors are joking around, showing up the foolishness of people, and Bruegel likes to do the same thing in his paintings. Last year he painted a picture called *Netherlandish Proverbs*, set in a village and illustrating as many Dutch proverbs as he could fit in. Among the scenes are a man carrying a basket of light into the sunshine – a pointless exercise – while another tries to make ends meet by stretching his arms between two loaves of bread. *Netherlandish Proverbs* led Bruegel on to paint *Children's Games*, which he has just finished.

✳ look at this

These children are playing blind man's buff. Look at how Bruegel paints them – they look like miniature adults, in the same type of clothes their parents wear when working in the fields. Bruegel hasn't painted portraits of particular children. He seems more interested in painting individual games than individual children, doesn't he?

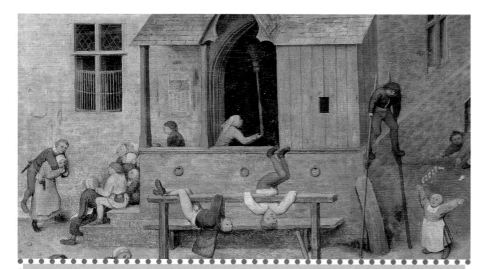

✳ look at this

This building looks important and may be the town hall. But there is so sign of the officials running the town. Instead, two boys are having great fun hanging upside-down on the beam outside, while a girl in the doorway concentrates on balancing a broom on the end of her finger. In this painting children are often shown playing games in places where adults should be working. Why do you think Bruegel has let children take over the town? And what is he trying to say? Perhaps he is suggesting that fun and games have a place in life, but if people are always clowning around enjoying themselves then nothing gets done.

DID YOU KNOW?

✳ The artist is now known as Pieter Bruegel the Elder because his son – also called Pieter – became a painter as well. The son is known as Pieter Bruegel the Younger.

✳ Bruegel the Elder liked to use unusual perspective techniques to give his paintings a strange, unsettling feeling.

✳ **Compare this**

Bruegel painted *Netherlandish Proverbs* a year before *Children's Games*, and packs a lot into this picture as well. He painted the scene as if looking down on a stage at a theatre, with people both near the front and far away. All the people in this village are shown doing silly things. In fact they are acting out proverbs or sayings, such as 'banging your head against a brick wall' and 'throwing your money down the drain' (or in this case into the river). Can you spot any other proverbs?

WANT TO SEE MORE?

www.artyfactory.com/perspective_
drawing/perspective_14.htm
www.gamesmuseum.uwaterloo.ca/
VirtualExhibits/Brueghel/imgmap.html

*Portrait of Pieter Bruegel the Elder
by Aegidius Sadeler, 1606*

It was the dramatic society that gave Bruegel the idea of painting *Children's Games* as if the viewer is looking at the scene from above. He wanted to include two hundred children playing eighty games, and realized that the only way to fit them all in was to make the square they play in like a stage. The view from the society's first-floor window gave him the idea, as he stood looking down on children playing below.

Many of the ideas for *Children's Games* and *Netherlandish Proverbs* came from recent books on popular games and sayings published in Antwerp, now a huge city and a centre of international trade. Bruegel thinks of another book he has at home, Desiderius Erasmus's *In Praise of Folly*, which also inspired him. In this book the character representing Folly looks down on Earth and says, 'There is no show like it.… What a theatre. How strange are the actions of fools.' Bruegel, too, wants his viewers to look down on his characters and wonder why they are wasting their time in such ways.

As the play continues, Bruegel thinks more about *Children's Games*. Although the painting isn't that big, he has squeezed a lot into it. There are games he remembers from his childhood and games he has witnessed on the street. He has included girls dressing dolls and boys playing tug-of-war on each other's backs. There are spinning tops and hoops, stilts and balls. Children swim, do headstands, run and balance.

WHY DON'T YOU?

Try a different point of view. Photograph your schoolyard or street from high up, then use your photos to make a present-day Bruegel scene. You could include your friends playing modern games.

✳ Compare this

When Bruegel got married, he moved to the city of Brussels and slowly his work began to change. His landscapes now had fewer people in them – compare this painting to *Children's Games*. *Hunters in the Snow* comes from a series of paintings showing the months of the year. This one is thought to represent a chilly January. Look at the wind blowing the fire. It makes you shiver!

All games are a distraction from the seriousness of life. They are fine for children, he thinks, but he has painted many of his children to look like adults and placed them in adult locations such as the large official building across the square.

Bruegel learned a lot from the earlier painter Hieronymus Bosch, whose work is still very popular in Antwerp. Bosch painted nightmarish scenes of ghouls and monsters, something that Bruegel used to do as well, but rarely does now unless pushed to do so by Cock. In the past Cock has even turned Bruegel's drawings of monstrous fish and demons into prints, and signed them to make it look as if Bosch had done them! But now Bruegel prefers to concentrate on his new subjects.

The play ends and Bruegel can hear children playing in the street outside. He hopes he has included their game in his painting.

AN OLD WOMAN COOKING EGGS
Diego Velázquez

Diego Rodríguez de Silva y Velázquez (1599–1660) painted *An Old Woman Cooking Eggs*, considered one of his finest works, when he was just nineteen. Later he became court painter to the King of Spain and painted the royal family for nearly forty years.

In Spain a tavern selling cheap food and wine is called a *bodega*, which is why this type of painting is known as a *bodegone*. In the tavern kitchen, a young boy fetches a carafe of wine and a melon, while an old woman cooks eggs. Look at the shiny pan below the stove, the half-glazed jugs on the right of the picture and the soft fabric of the woman's scarf. Each reflects light differently and in this way Velázquez shows us if it is soft or hard, shiny or rough.

1618

Diego Velázquez takes a step back from his easel and looks at the painting on it. He is nineteen years old, but already a fully qualified painter living in the Spanish port of Seville. He has just finished painting *An Old Woman Cooking Eggs*, and is adding the final highlights to the terracotta cooking pot and the wine in the carafe. He uses white brushstrokes to suggest light falling on the reflective surfaces. He wants them to seem as lifelike as possible.

The boy standing behind the easel starts to shift his feet. Velázquez gives him a coin and he runs out of the door. He has been posing for the painting with an older woman, who now carefully puts the egg she is holding into the bowl on the table. She stands slowly and stretches. The two of them have been posing for Velázquez almost every day for two months now, and she is pleased when he says the painting is finished.

This painting is a *bodegone*, a type of picture that is popular in Spain. *Bodegones* are set in taverns or kitchens, and show lots of different types of food and drink as well as pots, pans and serving dishes. Velázquez likes painting *bodegones*. When he was younger, he learned how to paint by looking at everyday objects such as food and cooking pots.

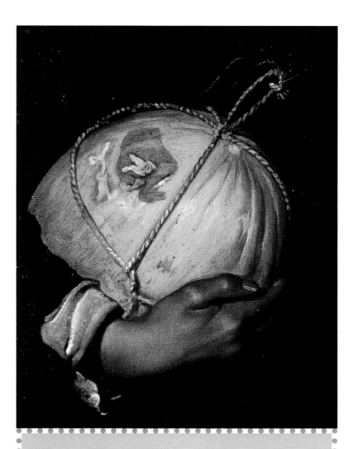

✳ look at this

Look how Velázquez has captured the moment when the raw eggs solidify in the cooking pot on the small stove by using bold brushstrokes of white paint. He contrasts these broad strokes with the almost photographic realism of the pot, which looks as if you could lift it out of the painting. In his later career as a court painter, he used the same techniques to paint the shimmer of the royal family's sumptuous clothes.

✳ look at this

Velázquez spent his teenage years training to be an artist. He often paid a local boy to pose for him so he could practise painting expressions. He would ask the boy to smile, frown, cry and laugh, and then try to capture each mood. Here he uses details such as the boy's reddened fingers to suggest that he serves people for a living but doesn't much enjoy it.

WHY DON'T YOU?

Make a papier-mâché melon! Cover a balloon in petroleum jelly. Then glue torn-up pieces of newspaper all over it with wallpaper paste. Let this dry for an hour or two, then repeat till there are three layers of newspaper. Put your melon aside to dry for a few days, then paint it.

*Self-portrait by
Diego Velázquez, aged 57*

But now he also paints stories from the Bible. He is lucky that he is allowed to do this – only the best painters in Seville are given a licence to paint religious scenes.

Velázquez did his first religious painting when he was only seventeen, but by then he had been training for six years, and his teacher, the artist Francisco Pacheco, said that he was already a better painter than himself. He lived and worked with Pacheco for six years, from the age of eleven until he was seventeen. They like each other a lot, and a few months ago he married Pacheco's fifteen-year-old daughter Juana.

This year Velázquez has received a big commission to complete two religious paintings for a convent in Seville, but his *bodegones* are also in demand and he is starting to build a reputation for himself. People admire his ability to paint things realistically, and the way he brings his work to life by contrasting smooth surfaces with rough ones and small brushstrokes with bold ones. He looks at the surface of *An Old Woman Cooking Eggs* and is pleased with the way the poached eggs seem to swirl in the pot, and how the gleam on the mortar and pestle contrasts with the dull shine of the melon tucked under the boy's arm.

Other Spanish artists working in a similar style like to show how clever they are at painting various types of surfaces – wet fish, metal spoons, knobbly carrots, clear glass. Some of their works are copied from prints of still life paintings by Dutch artists. Velázquez's paintings are simpler and more realistic. He paints real people preparing real

✳ Compare this

Later in life Velázquez became chief painter to the King of Spain and painted his family, including his daughter, the Infanta (Princess) Margarita, many times. He used techniques he had perfected painting his *bodegones* to capture their shimmering dresses and costumes. Look at Margarita's white sleeves, and compare them to the eggs in the pot in *An Old Woman Cooking Eggs*. In both instances, Velázquez uses broad strokes of white paint to show how light reflects off their surfaces.

DID YOU KNOW?

✳ Velázquez was court painter to King Philip IV of Spain. Nobody else was allowed to paint the royal family.

✳ In 1649 Velázquez went to Italy to collect paintings and sculptures on behalf of King Philip, who wanted to establish a Spanish academy of art.

✳ Velázquez was made a knight of the Order of Santiago, and held the highest position at King Philip's court. When he got his knighthood, the cross was added to his chest in the artist portrait on the opposite page.

food and places everything against a dark background so that it stands out. In *An Old Woman Cooking Eggs*, he has contrasted youth and old age, painting the boy's plump face next to the hollow cheeks of the woman and his smooth fingers beside her swollen hands.

Velázquez lifts down the canvas and places a new, blank one in its place. As he does so, his young wife walks in. He knows her round, smooth belly means he will be a father soon. It is important that he keeps working to ensure they will have enough money for when the baby comes. Artists in Seville are not highly thought of, and are paid little better than blacksmiths or potters. Velázquez is already ambitious for more. He knows that one day he will have to journey to Madrid and compete with other artists for the patronage of the royal family. But for now, he smiles at Juana and asks her to call back the serving woman he has just finished painting. He thinks he will paint her again.

WANT TO SEE MORE?

www.diegovelazquez.org
www.velazquezgallery.com
www.abcgallery.com/V/velazquez/
velazquez.html

THE ART OF PAINTING
Johannes Vermeer

Johannes Vermeer (1632–1675) lived in Delft in the Netherlands and is famous for his tranquil scenes of interiors. This painting was his own favourite.

Vermeer only painted two or three works a year, so he didn't make much money and was often in debt. But he was so fond of this painting that he always refused to sell it, even when he was almost bankrupt. It shows him painting a young woman dressed to represent Clio, the Greek muse of history. Can you see any other objects in the painting that make you think of history?

1667

Johannes Vermeer is seated in front of his easel. A soft yellow light filters through the windows in his first-floor studio. It lights up the map on the wall and the white marble tiles of the floor. He has placed a sculpture of a face and a sketchbook on a table and they catch the light as well. The sculpture isn't by him, and he doesn't use a sketchbook, but he has arranged them like this because he wants to include them in his latest painting. He is trying to create a picture that includes all the visual arts – painting, drawing, sculpture – in one ambitious work.

Vermeer is thirty-five years old and already has a reputation as one of the greatest painters in the Netherlands. He lives in Delft and has just been asked to be the governor of the painters' guild. He has already held this position once, five years ago, and it is a great honour to be asked again.

In addition to highlighting his talent as a painter of interiors, Vermeer wants this picture to connect him with the great artists of the past. That is why he is going to include himself, dressed in a medieval-style doublet (jacket) and pantaloons (knee-length, baggy trousers). The young woman he is painting is dressed as Clio, the Greek muse of history. She stands facing the studio window, wearing a blue wrap and holding a large yellow book. Vermeer places a wreath of laurel leaves on her head and hands her a trumpet. He knows that people seeing this painting will be able to tell who she represents from these symbols. Hanging on the wall behind her, a map of the Netherlands emphasizes his link to his country's artistic heritage.

As he picks up his square-tipped brush and starts to paint the model's blue wrap, Vermeer thinks about his finances. He wants this painting to be good because he really needs to make some money. For nearly ten years, he and his wife Catharina have been living with her mother, Maria Thins, in order to save money, but they are still in debt. Every time he sells a painting, it seems, they have another child and all the money goes on the baby. It is useful having his studio at his mother-in-law's house, because she has lots of expensive things like maps and paintings and furniture, which he can use as props in his paintings. But he sometimes finds it hard to concentrate with so many people about.

✳ look at this

Vermeer's paintings are often very detailed – almost like photographs – and he probably used a device called a 'camera obscura' to help him. But when you look closely, you can see his brushstrokes and the way he blended colours together. Look at Clio's shoulder – on her wrap you can see patches of blue, yellow, white and grey. Vermeer often used these colours in his paintings. Where else can you find them?

DID YOU KNOW?

✳ Vermeer and his wife Catharina had fifteen children!

✳ Vermeer loved to use ultramarine, an incredibly expensive blue pigment made from a stone called lapis lazuli. 'Ultramarine' means 'from across the sea' because the stone had to be imported from Afghanistan.

This painting of a maid pouring milk from a jug into a dish shows the bare walls and plain windows of the lower floor of Maria Thins's house. Can you see the broken window pane? Once again Vermeer has used his favourite colours of yellow and blue – compare the maid's dress to Clio's costume in *The Art of Painting*. He has also employed the same technique he used for the chandelier to highlight the milk jug, dish and bread in this painting.

WANT TO SEE MORE?

www.essentialvermeer.com
www.vermeer-foundation.org
www.bbc.co.uk/history/british/empire_seapower/vermeer_camera_01.shtml

Self-portrait by Johannes Vermeer, aged 24

Just this morning he lost his temper because two of his children had sneaked into his studio and moved things around. He had to spend ages rearranging the carpet he had suspended like a curtain and repositioning the stool. Luckily he had outlined the scene on his canvas the day before using his camera obscura, and he could use this device again to get things back to how they had been.

Vermeer's camera obscura is a small, darkened room at the back of the studio with a lens in one wall. Light from the studio passes through the lens to project an image of the studio interior onto the opposite wall. Vermeer can then place his canvas against the wall and trace an outline of the image in chalk. Working like this saves him a great deal of time and effort, and makes calculating perspective much easier. He used the camera obscura to work out the composition of this painting and to arrange his props – such as the chair at the front and the map at the back – so they line up with the edges of the canvas.

Vermeer works well today, painting the model's wrap in patches of blue, yellow, grey and white. He highlights the edge of her sleeve and collar. Looking up, he sees how the sunlight is making the brass gleam on the chandelier above her. He touches his painted version to see if it's dry, then swaps to a fine-pointed brush and starts to apply highlights carefully to each arm and candle-holder.

Suddenly he hears the woman posing as Clio gasp, and looks up just in time to see one of his daughters dart out of the door. She must have been hiding under the table the whole time, the model says. Vermeer frowns, and pushes a chair against the door so they won't be disturbed again. The light is already fading and there is still much to be done.

✳ Compare this

Vermeer painted in a room in his mother-in-law's house, so most of his paintings show her home and her possessions. Look at the floor in this painting – it's the same as the one in *The Art of Painting*. He also arranged many of his interior scenes in a similar way. Here, as in *The Art of Painting*, he uses a patterned carpet in the foreground and shows a man seated with his back to us. This man is listening to one woman sing while another plays the harpsichord. Even though we can't see his face we can tell he is sitting quietly. By contrast, the self-portrait of Vermeer in *The Art of Painting* is all action.

WHY DON'T YOU?

Create your own camera obscura. Make a room completely dark, using blackout material to ensure no light is visible through windows or doors. With a pin, make a tiny hole in the material covering the window. Hold a sheet of paper up to catch the light coming through the hole. You should see a dim, moving, upside-down, colour image of the world outside.

THE SKATE
Jean-Baptiste-Siméon Chardin

Jean-Baptiste-Siméon Chardin (1699–1779) was recognized as the best still life painter of his generation because of the way he made his subjects seem so realistic. His masterpiece *The Skate* helped to establish his reputation.

Chardin first exhibited *The Skate* at the Young Painters' Exhibition in Paris in 1727. It showed off his skill as a still life painter and was highly praised, securing him a place as an Academician at the famous Académie Royale (Royal Academy). Chardin gave the painting to the Academy when he joined. Look at the different surfaces reproduced in the painting – the folds in the cloth, the gleam of the skate's skin, the shine on the jug.

1728

It is 25 September and Jean-Baptiste-Siméon Chardin is standing outside the Académie Royale in Paris. He has an appointment there but he's early, so he walks up and down outside to pass the time. He has been asked to appear before the membership council of the Academy so they can decide if he should be allowed to join. The Academy is the best place in the country to study art, and for an artist to become a full member – an Academician – is to receive an official stamp of approval. Chardin longs to be an Academician one day, but for now he will be happy to be admitted as an Associate. In time this should help him become an Academician – and then, he hopes, people will admire his work and buy it.

The Academy ranks different types of painting in order of importance, the most respected category being history painting. Chardin had once hoped to become a history painter, but this requires special training. A history painter has to study at the Academy, and learn Greek and Latin as well. Instead, Chardin learned to draw and paint in other artists' studios, where he was taught to paint still lifes – arrangements of dead or inanimate objects such as jugs, cutlery, fruit

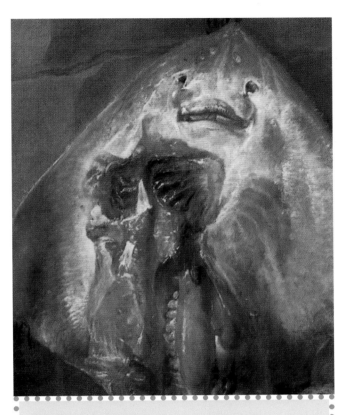

✳ Look at this

The central image of the skate hanging from a hook has transfixed viewers ever since it was painted. We can tell that the fish is dead, because it is out of water and its insides are visible. Chardin has painted the underside of the skate – the part that glides over the seabed – and we can make out its mouth and gills, but not its eyes, which are on the other side. Nonetheless, it seems to be staring at us and smiling, which is why it intrigues people.

DID YOU KNOW?

✳ The French writer Marcel Proust described the inside of Chardin's skate as like 'a multicoloured cathedral'.

✳ Chardin once said: 'Who told you that one paints with colours? One makes use of colours, but one paints with emotions.'

✳ Look at this

Do you think this cat has been nibbling on the skate? Or perhaps on the oysters it is standing on? Perhaps it has just been caught, as it looks startled, with its coat bristling, its back and tail raised and its ears pricked. Look at the cat's fur – it is soft and blurred, as if moving. Chardin didn't often paint living creatures – for one thing, they didn't keep still, and as he liked to paint slowly and deliberately this didn't really suit him.

Possible self-portrait by Jean-Baptiste-Siméon Chardin, aged 72

and fish. In the Academy's ranking, still life comes right at the bottom. But Chardin is lucky to have become an artist at all – his father had wanted him to work in the family business, making billiard tables.

Chardin now enjoys painting his still lifes. He carefully arranges the objects on a table, noting how the light from his studio window makes the glasses sparkle and the cooking pots gleam. He likes painting the different materials things are made from and trying to make them seem as real as possible, as if you could reach out and touch them. It is one of his still life paintings that has him pacing up and down outside the Academy now.

The Skate is very big for a still life, over a metre high (just over three feet) and almost a metre and a half wide (just under five feet). He painted it in his studio a couple of years ago. On the right of a table top Chardin arranged a selection of kitchen objects – a jug, a bottle, a cooking pot, a bowl, a knife, a cloth. On the left he placed two fish, three spring onions and a few oysters. Above the centre of the table he suspended a metal hook. On this he hung a fresh skate from the fish market, peeling back the smooth underbelly to show its insides. Within hours his studio had smelled like the market. Finally he added the cat, its arched back and pricked ears and tail adding life to the painting.

✳ Compare this

Look at how much simpler this painting is when compared with *The Skate*. As Chardin aged, his still lifes contained fewer pieces, placed in very bare settings. This allowed him to concentrate on painting the unique qualities of each item. Notice how he uses light to reveal the solidness of the coffee pot, the papery skin of the onions and the clear water in the transparent glass.

WANT TO SEE MORE?

www.jean-baptiste-simeon-chardin.org
www.artinthepicture.com/artists/Jean-Baptiste-Simeon_Chardin
www.ibiblio.org/wm/paint/auth/chardin

Chardin had chosen the objects in *The Skate* carefully and painted them in a range of browns, mixing the colours on his palette then blending them on the canvas with his brush and, at times, his thumb. He used white paint to highlight the cloth and the cat. But it was the skate that he wanted to stand out, its smooth underside luminescent and ghostly, its wings slightly bent like outstretched arms and its mouth and gills curled to resemble eyes and a mouth. Chardin meant to attract the Academy's attention with this painting.

He had kept *The Skate* in the studio for a while before an opportunity came up to exhibit it at the Young Painters' Exhibition in the Place Dauphine last June. The exhibition is held just once a year, outdoors, and for only six hours, but it teems with visitors. The size of the painting and the vivid red entrails of the fish made sure it stood out, and people were amazed by how realistically Chardin had painted the different elements of the picture. Some people found the skate a bit gory, but it had done the trick.

Suddenly the artist's thoughts are interrupted by a man asking if he is Monsieur Chardin. He nods, and follows the man into the Academy and up to the room where the membership council are sitting. As he enters, he sees a man lean towards his neighbour and hears him whisper that this kind of decision is very rare, and that it has only happened once before. What can he mean?

Chardin stands in front of the council and waits to hear if they have decided to make him an Associate Member. It means so much to him, and he desperately hopes they will say yes. A council member stands up. 'Monsieur Chardin,' he says, 'we have decided to make you an Associate Member of this fine Academy.' Chardin smiles, but the man has not finished speaking. 'And,' he continues, 'owing to your exceptional talent at painting animals and fruit, and on condition that you give the Academy your painting *The Skate* and a further painting of a fruit buffet, we also have pleasure in making you a full Academician as well.' Chardin lets out his breath. Official recognition at last!

* compare this

Chardin's still lifes were mainly bought by close friends and other artists, and for a while he tried to rise in the Academy's ranking by painting living things. Genre scenes like this one were popular among the royal families of Europe. Here a young girl carries a racquet and shuttlecock as if she is about to play, but she is fashionably dressed as an adult – her hair has been coloured grey with powder and she wears a flowered cap.

WHY DON'T YOU?

Engage your senses. When people look at Chardin's painting, they think they can smell the fish. Place an item such as a peeled onion or scented flower into a clean glass jar. Ask a friend to close their eyes, sniff the jar, then draw what they have smelled. Take it in turns. Ask your friend to give you something to smell and draw. See how often you guess right, and how well your drawings compare to the objects.

Self-Portrait Hesitating Between the Arts of Music and Painting

Angelica Kauffman

Angelica Kauffman (1741–1807) was one of the most successful portrait painters of the eighteenth century. She worked in Italy and England and turned the world 'Angelicamad' for her fashionable portraits of the aristocracy.

Throughout her life Angelica Kauffman painted herself. In this painting she shows the two loves of her life, music and painting, in the form of two women. Both the women seem to plead with the central figure, who is Kauffman herself. While she looks at Music, we can see she has made up her mind to go with Painting, though it seems to have been a hard choice.

1794

Angelica Kauffman enters her studio as the large grandfather clock in the hall strikes four. She bought the clock in London and it always reminds her of the fifteen years she spent there, being celebrated as the most fashionable portrait painter in town. She still paints English people, even though she hasn't lived in London for over ten years. That's because so many of them holiday in Rome, Italy, where she now lives with her husband. She has just returned from seeing a friend, the young English novelist Cornelia Knight, whom she recently painted, and they have spent the morning talking about her time in London.

Kauffman shuts her studio door and breathes in the smell of oil paint. The room is full of jars of oil, easels and palettes, and she loves it. She is never happier than when she is working, and she now busies herself selecting a canvas for the new portrait she will begin tomorrow. She pauses for a moment to look at the finished self-portrait still on her easel and smiles. The painting doesn't show Kauffman as she is now, but as she was when she was about Cornelia's age. Kauffman is over fifty now, and has often painted herself. As a young woman she portrayed herself in the national costume of her father's home town in Germany, as if emphasizing her roots – even though she was born in Switzerland and grew up in Austria.

In the painting she has just finished, *Self-Portrait Hesitating Between the Arts of Music and Painting*, Kauffman appears between two female figures representing the things she loved best as a young woman – music and painting. Music sits in a red dress with a sheet of music in her lap, while Painting holds a palette and brushes and points into the distance. Each seems to be asking Kauffman to choose her. Music sits holding her hand and gazing at her with pleading eyes, while Painting is all action, her hand pointing to the future and her palette already prepared. Kauffman has painted the moment she chose art, rather than singing, as her future career. She really did have to make this choice when she was starting out, but that was a long time ago now. She started painting portraits for money when she was only twelve, and by twenty-one she was a full member of the prestigious Florence Art

✳ look at this

Kauffman was fifty-three years old when she painted this. Do you think she looks that age? It seems she has painted herself as a young woman. When she was young she had to make a choice as to whether to be a painter or a singer, as she had a very good voice but was also excellent at painting portraits. Look at the expression of her eyes and mouth. It is as if she is saying sorry to Music just by looking in her direction.

WHY DON'T YOU?

Try drawing or painting a self-portrait. You could use a mirror or copy a photograph of yourself. Try to include some objects that will say something about you – your pets, some of your favourite books or games, or things representing music, sports or movies you enjoy.

This portrait of the British actor David Garrick is one of Kauffman's most famous works, and was painted in Naples when he was on holiday there. In 1765, the year before she moved to England, she sent the finished portrait to an exhibition in London. It attracted a lot of attention and ensured people were keen for her to paint them as soon as she arrived. Compare this picture to Kauffman's self-portrait. Her painting of David Garrick doesn't tell a story, but rather tries to show the man behind all the characters he played on stage. He was famous for his expressive eyes and face. Do you think she has captured them well?

DID YOU KNOW?

* Kauffman was close friends with the English artist Sir Joshua Reynolds, and they painted each other's portraits.

* David Garrick thought her as good a singer as the best in London, and the German writer Goethe called her 'the most accomplished woman in Europe'.

Academy and about to move to Rome, where she could secure even bigger commissions.

In Rome there were more opportunities for her to shine as a portrait artist, and she also spent time in Naples, where wealthy foreigners came on holiday. It was fashionable for members of British high society to make a 'Grand Tour' of Europe, visiting Italy to see Roman architecture, Greek sculpture, and paintings by Leonardo and Botticelli. While they were there, they had time to have their portraits painted, and Kauffman was a popular choice. She also began painting scenes from Greek and Roman history to sell to the visitors, but it was her portraits that made her stand out.

While in Naples, Kauffman painted the famous English actor David Garrick, and in 1865 she sent the portrait to be exhibited in London. It was an immediate success and she decided to move to England. Soon she was busy with commissions, and ended up painting Queen Charlotte and many other noblewomen. Connoisseurs praised her ability to capture not just the outward appearance of her subjects, but also their inner character.

Kauffman spent an amazing fifteen years in London. When her father joined her there, he saw society going 'Angelicamad' for her paintings and prints. Pottery companies such as Wedgwood reproduced her paintings on tea sets, and she was much in demand as a portraitist. But in the end she returned to Rome, where she painted portraits of travelling English nobility and an occasional self-portrait.

She looks at her self-portrait again. Everyone knows she chose painting over music, although she still loves to sing and play the harpsichord. In this painting she has enjoyed combining her skill at portraiture with her love of classical history and mythology. That is why she has shown Music sitting by the Doric columns of an ancient building while Painting points to a classical temple on a distant hill. The three figures in the painting – Music, Painting and herself – look like the Three Graces who represented beauty and creativity in Greek mythology. But Music and Painting also offer her the choice of Hercules between an easy, pleasure-filled life (represented by Music) and the hard but worthwhile path indicated by Painting.

Kauffman knows self-portraits are often used by artists to prove how good they are at likenesses, but she didn't paint this work for that reason. She wants to show how she can fuse an understanding of Greek mythology with her skill for painting people and portraits. And if she has had to paint herself looking thirty years younger in order to tell her story, then so be it.

Self-portrait by Angelica Kauffman, aged 12

✳ Compare this

Kauffman painted this double portrait of Anna Maria Jenkins and Thomas Jenkins in Rome, where Jenkins worked as an art dealer and banker. The young woman is his niece, and she wants to get married. The painting is meant to show off her beauty, her figure and her family's position (Kauffman's portraits were not cheap). Compare Miss Jenkins with Kauffman in her self-portrait. Both women wear white dresses, but the way they are shown seems to tell us different things about themselves. Miss Jenkins stands still and holds a flower garland, trying to look pretty and gentle to attract a husband. Kauffman has painted herself at the same age, but shows herself as a free spirit, making her own decisions about her life.

WANT TO SEE MORE?

http://hoocher.com/Angelika_Kauffmann/
Angelica_Kauffmann.htm
www.angelica-kauffmann.de/e/index.shtml

THE MONK BY THE SEA
Caspar David Friedrich

The Monk by the Sea and its companion painting The Abbey in the Oak Wood secured the reputation of Caspar David Friedrich (1774–1840) as one of the leading Romantic artists in Europe. Designed to be seen together, these two paintings capture Friedrich's fascination with painting nature as a way of expressing his inner feelings.

This painting is almost abstract. Only the standing figure diverts our attention from the three bands of colour – the pale white sand dunes, the blue-black sea and the sky that subtly changes all the way up the canvas.

Look how these bands of colour continue in the companion painting *The Abbey in the Oak Wood*, and how the storm in the top right corner of *The Monk by the Sea* extends into the top left corner of this painting. This one is almost monochrome, executed in a single colour. The sky, the snowy ground, the monks, the trees, the ruin and the cross under the arch are all painted in tones of brown. A thick fog has descended and threatens to make the monks disappear from view. How do these two paintings make you feel?

1811

Caspar David Friedrich enters his studio and closes the door. He has just discovered that he's been elected a member of the Berlin Art Academy. This is a great honour, and he doesn't want anyone disturbing him while he takes in the news. Friedrich lives in the city of Dresden (now in Germany), but last year he sent a pair of paintings – *The Monk by the Sea* and *The Abbey in the Oak Wood* – to the Academy's exhibition in Berlin. Their success is why he has been asked to join the Academy.

He knows it was a close vote, as many of the artists who are already members don't like his way of painting. They prefer artists to paint what they see in front of them, a style called 'Naturalism'. Friedrich also paints nature, but he uses things he has seen and sketched outdoors – mountains, storms, forests, seas – to create paintings that reflect what he is feeling inside. People call this style of painting 'Romanticism'. Friedrich thinks there is no point in painting landscapes if they don't reveal something of the painter as well.

He takes down a clean wooden palette from where it hangs on the wall. He is halfway through a painting of a winter landscape and wants to work on it while there is still enough daylight. Friedrich is thirty-six, but has only been painting for four years, even though he has studied art since he was fourteen. For a long time he made neat, detailed drawings of trees, rocks and fields. He even won an important art prize with them. But it wasn't until he started painting his big landscapes that he received widespread recognition. Now royalty buy his paintings. The Crown Prince of Prussia, who is fifteen years old, persuaded his father to buy *The Monk by the Sea* and *The Abbey in the Oak Wood* for him after seeing them at the Berlin Art Academy exhibition.

Friedrich remembers when these paintings were still in his studio. He painted them to hang together, and each has three distinct bands of colour across it. In *The Monk by the Sea*, the sparsely tufted sand dunes offer a view of the dark blue sea behind, with a stormy horizon stretching up to a blue sky above. There seems to be no end to the sea or the sky. When we look at this boundless space, it can make us feel as small and insignificant as the tiny figure standing on the sand.

✳ look at this

Up close you can see Friedrich's sandy hair and know that he has painted himself into this picture. But it really doesn't matter who is standing there. Seen from the back, the figure in its dark monk's habit could be anyone – even you. The scale of the figure allows Friedrich to show us how small a person is compared to the endless landscape.

WANT TO SEE MORE?

www.caspardavidfriedrich.org
http://smarthistory.org/friedrich-monk-by-the-sea.html

Self-portrait by Caspar David Friedrich, aged 36

The figure is in fact a painting of Friedrich himself, dressed as a monk (you can tell it is him by the colour of his sandy hair). Imagine painting yourself so small, and the sky and sea so big they seem to stretch on forever. Friedrich is showing how he feels when confronted by the vastness of nature. This sense of nature overpowering mankind is called the 'Sublime'.

Friedrich's works are very different from the paintings of other landscape artists, who carefully arrange trees, rocks and rivers to create attractive scenes. Friedrich isn't interested in prettiness – he wants to make his audience think about huge topics such as life and death.

Friedrich knows that not everyone cares for his paintings. The famous writer Johann Wolfgang von Goethe declared them so empty of content that it wouldn't matter which way up you hung them, while the novelist Heinrich von Kleist said no place on earth could be sadder than where the monk stood. But other people do like them. The doctor Carl Gustav Carus thought *The Abbey in the Oak Wood* was the most poetic landscape painting he had ever seen.

✻ Compare this

Can you find the ship in this painting? It is being crushed by the jagged peaks of ice that stretch as far as the eye can see. Friedrich has included it to emphasize the power of nature and its ability to dwarf and crush mankind. In this way, the ship is similar to the monk in *The Monk by the Sea*. It allows Friedrich to paint the power and beauty of nature and to express how it makes him feel.

<h2>✳ Compare this</h2>

The focus of this painting is the figure of a man who has climbed to the top of a rocky outcrop and now stands looking down at the landscape beneath him. Mist lies in the valley and wind swirls through his distinctive sandy-coloured hair, telling us that this is another of Friedrich's self-portraits. Once again, he has his back to us, as if inviting us to stand by him and contemplate the sublime landscape before us.

DID YOU KNOW?

✳ Romantic artists like Friedrich wanted to experience the grandeur of nature. They liked to go for long walking holidays in the mountains and made hiking a popular pastime.

✳ Friedrich was known as very serious and melancholy, but letters to his friends show he also had a sense of humour.

✳ When he was a child, many members of his family died. Do you think this might have been the reason he was often sad?

WHY DON'T YOU?

Write a Romantic poem or piece of music. Romanticism wasn't just about painting. Composers like Beethoven and poets like Keats also tried to express their feelings of the Sublime through their music or words.

Friedrich sighs and sits down in front of his easel. He rubs his eyes, and tries to forget about the paintings – they belong to the Crown Prince of Prussia now. He needs to finish the winter landscape he dreamed up during his last walking trip in the mountains. To remember how he felt as he crunched through the deep snow he needs to close his eyes....

THE RAFT OF THE MEDUSA
Théodore Géricault

Théodore Géricault (1791–1824) died when he was just thirty-two years old. This huge canvas was his masterpiece. It shows a group of men stranded on a raft after the sinking of their ship off the coast of Africa. At this moment they have just seen another ship on the horizon and hope it will spot them and come to their rescue.

This enormous work is on a scale normally only used for commissioned history paintings, but Géricault wasn't paid to paint it. He was lucky his father was wealthy enough to pay for his studio and materials, and to support him while he was painting it. To help him in his work, he talked with and sketched the survivors of the actual shipwreck.

1819

Théodore Géricault is lying on his bed with his eyes shut. Every time he opens his eyes he sees the giant canvas he has just finished painting. It is in his studio and part of it is visible through the open doorway of the bedroom. *The Raft of the Medusa* is seven metres wide (twenty-three feet) and five metres tall (sixteen and a half feet), and it is the biggest thing he has ever painted. It has taken all his energy to finish it. Now he lies motionless on his bed in the room next to the studio, where he has been eating and sleeping for the past eight months.

Géricault moved to this large studio in the Faubourg du Roule district of Paris, France, last November. Nearby, the half-built Arc de Triomphe is taking shape. Géricault had been living at his father's house but decided to move somewhere quieter, where he wouldn't be distracted, to complete this painting. His father has paid for the new studio, for all his paints and for the vast roll of canvas he needed. Usually artists only ever work on this scale when someone else is paying, for such a project is both expensive and time-consuming. Géricault knows he is lucky that his father has money, because he has painted something that he doubted anyone would have commissioned. It is his masterpiece.

He slowly pulls himself up to a sitting position on the bed and reaches over to the table for a piece of bread. He is thinking about why he decided to paint *The Raft of the Medusa* in the first place.

Two years ago, Géricault had returned from a trip to Italy to find everyone talking about a shipwreck that had happened the year before, but was still in the news. The *Medusa* had been the flagship of a small French convoy bound for Senegal in West Africa. The captain hadn't been to sea for over twenty years, and had only been given his position because he had influential friends in the government. He wasn't a very good sailor, and when he grounded the ship on a sand bank just out of sight of the coast of Africa he couldn't get it off again. After three days it started to break up and he took the decision to abandon ship. But instead of making sure all his crew and passengers safely reached the shore, he quickly hopped into the best lifeboat with a few of his senior officers and sailed away.

✱ look at this

When Géricault was planning *The Raft of the Medusa* he made a lot of studies showing the figures on the raft with the ship coming to rescue them. In the first sketches the ship was much larger, but as he came nearer to painting the finished work he kept making it smaller and smaller. Why do you think he did this? It could be that he wanted to add drama to the painting as the men strain to see the far-off ship and attract its attention, even while the wind in their sail is taking them away from it.

WHY DON'T YOU?

Illustrate a dramatic event from the news. It doesn't have to be a tragedy – it could be a sporting victory or a big celebration. The important thing is to include lots of action.

DID YOU KNOW?

✳ The famous painter Eugène Delacroix posed for one of the dying figures in Géricault's masterpiece.

✳ As a boy, Géricault was fascinated by horses, and they became one of his favourite subjects. He was a keen rider to the end of his life, though he suffered several riding accidents.

✳ A carving of his great masterpiece appears on his tomb, beneath a bronze figure of the artist.

✳ Compare this

This chalk drawing is one of many sketches and studies Géricault completed in preparation for painting *The Raft of the Medusa*. It shows one of the shipwreck survivors, Alexandre Corréard. Look at Géricault's fast and confident sketching style. Can you find this figure in the painting? In the sketch you can tell that Corréard is posing in the studio – he doesn't look as worried or anxious as Géricault has painted him in the finished work, does he?

There wasn't room for the remaining crew and passengers in the remaining lifeboats, so a makeshift raft was constructed and 150 men climbed aboard. The lifeboats were supposed to tow the raft to the shore, but it was too heavy. Soon the raft and everyone on it were abandoned and left to drift. Those on board had no way of steering the raft and little to eat or drink. The waves were high and they were permanently wet. Finally, after thirteen days, another ship from the convoy spotted the raft and rescued the survivors.

After Géricault heard this story, he read a book about the shipwreck written by two of the survivors, Alexandre Corréard and Henri Savigny, and knew this was the subject he had been looking for. Previously, he had painted soldiers and their horses, but this new subject stirred him. He felt passionately that the captain had been wrong to abandon his men to their fate, and he started to plan a painting of the raft.

Géricault contacted the authors and other survivors, meeting up with them and sketching them for the painting. He had a scale model of the raft built and posed wax figurines on it. He travelled to Le Havre, on the coast near his home town of Rouen, to paint the waves and coastal clouds. He sketched sick people in hospital and even studied dead bodies. And he painted endless variations on the theme of men on a raft, from them climbing on to their being rescued. Eventually he chose to paint the moment when they have seen a ship on the horizon and desperately try to catch the lookout's attention by shouting and waving.

During last summer Géricault perfected the composition and moved to his new studio, where he had enough space to stretch his giant canvas and to work in peace. He had all but locked himself in, eating and drinking in the studio. He'd even had all his hair cut off so it wouldn't bother him. He wanted to live and breathe the raft, to smell the salt water crashing down and to feel the men's overriding desire to survive against the odds.

Géricault had painted quickly, moving from one figure to another until they were all finished. He had grouped the figures together, many of them mirroring each other's poses, their outstretched hands reaching for the ship they could see in the distance. Then he started adding shadows to link the figures together, using thick bitumen instead of black paint to make them as dark and rich as possible. He wanted the greatest possible contrast between the men on the raft and the ghostly suggestion of sails on the horizon, the faint glimmer of hope they now clung to. Were they going to be rescued, or was the ship going to pass them by? The wind that filled their small sail and tugged at their hair suggested it would take them in the wrong direction, and they could only hope the ship would see them and come to their aid.

Géricault falls back on his bed again, exhausted. Even thinking about the painting makes him feel tired, and he closes his eyes. Tomorrow he will have to work out how to transport it to the Louvre for the Salon exhibition. But for now he must sleep.

Portrait of Théodore Géricault by Alexandre Colin, 1824

✳ compare this

Géricault was just twenty-one when this painting of a cavalry officer in the heat of battle was exhibited at the Paris Salon. *The Charging Chasseur* was the first of his paintings to be accepted and it won a gold medal. Seven years later *The Raft of the Medusa* also won a gold medal. Which painting do you prefer?

WANT TO SEE MORE?

www.visual-arts-cork.com/famous-artists/ gericault-theodore.htm
http://wapedia.mobi/en/Théodore_Géricault

THE HAY WAIN
John Constable

John Constable (1776–1837) is now England's most famous landscape artist, but he sold fewer than twenty paintings in his home country during his own lifetime. He painted the Suffolk countryside of his childhood throughout his life, adding dramatic skies to scenes of rural life and reinvigorating the art of landscape painting. *The Hay Wain* is his most popular work.

The Hay Wain shows a scene Constable would have witnessed every year as a boy – the gathering in of hay. In the distance a hay wain can be seen, fully loaded. An empty cart will be needed soon, and two men are bringing one across the millstream at the ford, a shallow crossing place in the river. A man called Willie Lott lives in the house on the left. Flatford Mill, owned by Constable's father, was behind the artist as he sketched this view.

1824

It is a few days before Christmas, and John Constable is writing to his friend John Fisher, the Archdeacon of Salisbury Cathedral. He is telling him about a painting he finished three years ago that is now being exhibited in Paris, France. It is a large painting of a cart crossing a river by a ford, heading for the fields beyond. He originally called it *Landscape: Noon* but the Archdeacon soon started calling it *The Hay Wain*, as did everyone else.

The Hay Wain is on display at the Salon, an important exhibition held every year. Constable tells his friend that it has recently been moved to a better position within the exhibition because it is so popular, and that many French artists – including the famous Romantic painter Eugène Delacroix – have been impressed by his ability to bring the landscape to life in paint. He doesn't hold back in praising his own work. After all, it has taken long enough for his paintings to be appreciated. When he first showed *The Hay Wain* at the Royal Academy's summer exhibition in London, nobody bought it, and it took over two years to sell.

Landscape painting is not highly regarded in England at the moment. Grand paintings of historical events, Bible stories and classical myths dominate the summer exhibition, and people still want their portraits painted. Landscapes are mostly overlooked. Constable is determined to change that, and to see landscape ranked alongside the other grand subjects at the Royal Academy. He wants to follow in the footsteps of

✱ look at this

In the far distance, a group of farm labourers are cutting down the hay with scythes. Using many different shades of green, Constable suggests richly varied woodland behind the men. The full hay cart can be seen among the trees (look for its wheels). The 'master of the harvest' – the person in charge of gathering the hay – wears a red sash. Constable was not a precise painter and often used just a couple of brushstrokes to suggest a branch or a body.

✱ look at this

The river not only provided power for the mill, but also water for people living along the banks in houses such as Willie Lott's. Here a woman bends down at the end of a small jetty to reach the water. Someone else is lurking on the far bank of the river, behind a family of ducks. What do you think he is hoping to pull out of the water?

WHY DON'T YOU?

Try skywatching. The sky was important in Constable's paintings, and he made endless sketches of clouds. You could try taking a photograph of the sky every day at the same time and in the same place. Did you realize how much the sky changes? You could mount your pictures together on the wall, or make an album.

WANT TO SEE MORE?

www.john-constable.org
www.icons.org.uk/theicons/collection/
hay-wain/features

his heroes, the French landscape painters Claude Lorrain and Nicolas Poussin. That is why he now paints on large canvases measuring nearly two metres across (six and a half feet). Nobody can ignore his landscapes when they are so big, he reasons.

Constable wants to capture what nature is really like and bases all his 'six-footers' on sketches done outdoors, immersing himself in the landscape he has known all his life. He was born and grew up in East Bergholt, a small village in Suffolk, England. His father owned mills and land around the village, and Constable had an idyllic childhood playing on the banks of the river Stour. His father wanted him to go into the family business or the church, but Constable just wanted to go out sketching with his friend John Dunthorne, the local plumber. He did spend a year working for his father, but eventually he persuaded his family to let him become a painter. He moved to London and was accepted as a student at the Royal Academy.

It was lucky for Constable that his father was wealthy, as he hardly sold any paintings at first, and didn't even have enough money to get

✳ Compare this

A boy crouches down at the side of the river to untie the horse from the barge (a shallow river boat) it has been towing to allow it to pass under a footbridge. Constable's father not only owned Flatford Mill, but also the barges that were used to take the flour produced there to the coast for sale. Constable painted this four years before *The Hay Wain*, and hasn't added any white highlights to bring it to life. It is smaller than *The Hay Wain* and seems very still and calm by comparison, don't you think?

✳ Compare this

Constable was fascinated with clouds and described the sky as the most important part of a landscape painting when it came to creating a particular mood. He spent the summers of 1821 and 1822 painting the clouds he saw. He wrote on the back of many of his sketches. This one states: '5 Sep 1822 10 o clock Morng. Looking South-East. Very brisk wind at West. Very bright & fresh Grey Clouds running very fast over a yellow bed. about half way in the Sky very appropriate for the coast at Osmington.' Look at the sky in *The Hay Wain*. What kind of day is it? Do you think it is a good day to be collecting hay?

married. But that changed in 1816, after his father died and left him part of his estate, and now he can hear his wife Maria and his four young children moving about their house on Charlotte Street in London.

The light is fading, and Constable looks up from his letter. He notices the storm clouds gathering in the distance, while sunlight still falls on the garden. It reminds him of the changeable weather he painted in *The Hay Wain*, with clouds scudding across the sky, their shadows patterning the fields. Although he'd been very careful to make sure the hay wain and the figures were true to life – for reference, he'd used an accurate drawing of a hay cart sent to him by John Dunthorne's son – the landscape was the chief subject of the painting.

Constable had wanted the trees in the picture to appear as if they were moving in the breeze, their leaves paler where they were lit by the sun, and for the clouds to give a sense of energy to the scene. He wanted the shallow river to reflect the sunlight and to gleam and sparkle. To achieve this effect, he had used pure white paint, which critics of his work dubbed 'Constable's snow'. But he knew his techniques worked. Although the small details in the scene – the fisherman on the bank, the master of the harvest at work in the fields, the harness of the horses as they plod through the shallow water – are dwarfed by the landscape, Constable made them stand out by highlighting them in red. This made the surrounding green leaves appear even more vivid.

After painting *The Hay Wain*, Constable had spent two summers painting nothing but clouds, carefully noting down the time of day, the date and how windy it was. Now, he notes, the clouds are threatening rain, and he finishes his letter in the growing darkness.

*Self-portrait by
John Constable, aged 30*

A BURIAL AT ORNANS
Gustave Courbet

Gustave Courbet (1819–1877) was the most important Realist painter of the nineteenth century. His large paintings were considered shocking because they showed unknown people going about their everyday lives, rather than idealized stories, pretty places or celebrities.

Courbet moved back and forth between Paris and his home town of Ornans, where he saw and painted the hardship of people living off the land and working in the fields. At first his paintings surprised and upset some critics, who didn't know who these people were and didn't think they were doing anything particularly special.

DID YOU KNOW?

✳ Courbet was known as the leader of the Realist school of painting.

✳ He remained close to his family throughout his life, and included portraits of them in many of his paintings.

✳ He was offered the Légion d'Honneur, France's highest honour, by Emperor Napoleon III, but refused it because he disapproved of the regime.

1850

Low grey clouds hang over the small town of Ornans in eastern France as Gustave Courbet puts down his paintbrush. He normally lives and works in Paris, but he returned to his home town last autumn to paint the local people. Although it is nearly midday, his studio is dark and it is hard to see some of the detail on his latest painting, even though it fills an entire wall. He steps back as far as he can and looks at it. *A Burial at Ornans* is a giant group portrait of his family, friends and other local people. Each figure is life-size, and there are forty-five of them. It has been quite an undertaking.

The painting is nearly seven metres wide (twenty-three feet) and three and a half metres high (eleven and a half feet). In Courbet's small studio – a room in a house his parents own – it is difficult to get a sense of how it will look on the vast walls of the Louvre in Paris. He is going to show it at the Salon, the official art exhibition held there each year, and he wants it to dominate the room.

The other artists in the exhibition will have to submit their work to a selection committee, but last year Courbet won a gold medal for his painting *After Dinner at Ornans*, so this year he is allowed to send whatever he likes. He is going to send *A Burial at Ornans* and two other large paintings of people from the town. Courbet is pleased that he doesn't have to send his paintings to the selection committee any more, as they rejected them for years. But two years ago, in 1848, there was a revolution in France and people took to the streets, overthrew the government and deposed the king. France became a republic, and suddenly Courbet's paintings of working-class peasants were praised as revolutionary statements and accepted at the Salon.

Even though he has painted a religious occasion in *A Burial at Ornans,* it is not a religious painting of the kind normally seen at the Salon. It doesn't focus on Christ or Bible figures. Courbet has included a small carving of Christ on the cross, held high on a pole in the air, but it is overlooked – this painting is all about the earth and its people. Courbet never paints scenes from history, mythology or the Bible – the types of paintings that were traditionally seen as the best work in the Salon. He paints the everyday people of his home town, its priests and officials, his parents and the men and women who work on the land.

✳ look at this

The people in this painting all seem to be thinking about different things. What do you think these two choirboys are thinking about? One looks up at a priest, as if for advice or guidance. The other looks away from the crowd of people and the open grave in front of him. He seems lost in his own world. Many of the adults in the painting also seem preoccupied.

Self-portrait by Gustave Courbet, aged 29

Some, like his parents, are moderately wealthy and others incredibly poor. Some critics find these works difficult to accept, because Courbet paints peasants on the kind of huge canvases that in the past were reserved for historical or religious paintings.

Courbet came up with the idea for his latest painting at his grandfather's funeral. His sisters and parents were by the grave, as were many other people from the town, of all ages and from different walks of life. He was inspired by the way a funeral could bring all kinds of people together, and started to sketch out how the finished painting might look.

Courbet just wants to paint life as it is, with gritty honesty. He used to discuss his ideas with his friends at the Brasserie Andler, a café near his studio in Paris. His friends include the writers Charles Baudelaire and Jules Champfleury, who admire the realism of Courbet's paintings and call themselves 'Realists', a name Champfleury invented to emphasize their mutual interest in recording real life. People have started calling the Brasserie Andler 'the Temple of Realism'.

Courbet knows that not everyone likes looking at large paintings of working-class people doing basic things like eating or attending a funeral. He also knows that most of the people who see his paintings

✳ Compare this

This was Courbet's first large-scale painting to be set in Ornans, and shows a group of men listening to a fiddler while relaxing after a meal. Following the 1848 revolution, it was well received and won a gold medal at the 1849 Salon. Courbet used similar colours for much of *A Burial at Ornans*. He sometimes mixed sand with his paint to make it seem thicker, as if he was painting with the earth itself.

WANT TO SEE MORE?

www.musee.orsay.fr/en/collections/courbet-dossier/biography.html
http://cgfa.acropolisinc.com/courbet

in Paris have never heard of Ornans. But he wants to show these Parisian city people that life exists elsewhere. He wants to show the dignity of the gravedigger and the grief of the female mourners. He has included his three sisters crying into their handkerchiefs and a local revolutionary in his turquoise stockings. He has painted the boredom on the faces of the beadles (church officials) in their red robes and hats, and the dutiful expressions of the children.

Suddenly there is a knock at the studio door and Courbet's sister pokes her head into the room. 'Time to eat,' she says. Courbet, always partial to eating and drinking at any time of the day or night, follows her willingly towards their parents' house for lunch.

✳ Compare this

This giant painting is different from Courbet's other Realist works in that the scene is made up, and many of the people shown never posed for him. Set in his Paris studio, the painting tells the viewer about Courbet's life. The people he likes are shown on the right, and include his friends Baudelaire (sitting reading) and Champfleury (sitting on a chair). The people he doesn't like, including the Emperor Napoleon III (posed as a poacher with two dogs), are on the left. Courbet sits in the middle, painting a landscape. He exhibited this painting alongside *A Burial at Ornans* in 1855. It seems to have a much more complex message. Which painting do you prefer?

WHY DON'T YOU?

Paint a picture of a family occasion. It could be a big event like a wedding or holiday gathering, or just an ordinary mealtime. Try to capture each person's character in their pose and expression.

OPHELIA
John Everett Millais

John Everett Millais (1829–1896) was a child genius, the youngest ever student at London's Royal Academy. He enjoyed lifelong success, but his early paintings are regarded as his masterpieces. *Ophelia* was painted while he was a member of the group called the 'Pre-Raphaelite Brotherhood', who believed artists should paint directly from nature.

In Shakespeare's play *Hamlet*, Ophelia is the lover of Hamlet, the Prince of Denmark. When Hamlet kills her father and rejects her, Ophelia is driven mad with grief. Singing songs and carrying flower garlands, she wanders to a stream. While trying to hang the flowers in the branches of an overhanging willow, she falls into the water and, instead of saving herself, allows herself to drown. Critics found this painting too realistic when it was first exhibited, but it soon came to be Millais's most popular work.

1852

An early morning fog has cleared to leave a cloudless day as John Everett Millais walks into Trafalgar Square in London, England. He strides past the National Gallery and into the Royal Academy, whose annual summer exhibition has just opened to the public. Millais knows the Royal Academy very well, having studied in its school since the age of eleven. He is only twenty-two now, but his paintings regularly appear in the summer exhibition, and he is already well known. This is partly because of his precocious talent and partly because of his membership of the Pre-Raphaelite Brotherhood – a group of artists including his friends William Holman Hunt and Dante Gabriel Rossetti. He hopes his latest work, *Ophelia*, will cement his fame and make him a hugely successful painter.

Millais and his friends founded their Pre-Raphaelite Brotherhood in 1848 to try and escape the restrictive teachings of the Royal Academy. They felt the school over-emphasized the work of sixteenth-century painters like Raphael and their slickness of finish. They wanted to paint like earlier artists – to be 'pre-Raphael'. Millais, Hunt and Rossetti were also influenced by the famous art critic John Ruskin. In his book *Modern Painters*, Ruskin encouraged young British artists to 'go to nature in all singleness of heart…rejecting nothing, selecting nothing and scorning nothing'. Taking him at his word, they started painting outdoors.

Millais enters the Royal Academy and heads to the main exhibition room. The walls are crammed with pictures from floor to ceiling, but there is his own, hanging in the very best spot 'on the line' – at eye level.

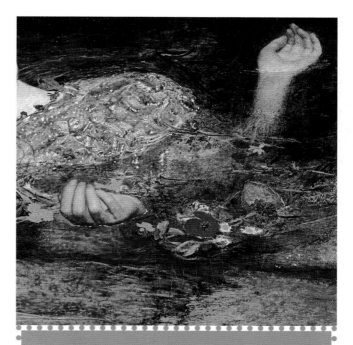

✳ look at this

In Victorian times, when Millais painted *Ophelia*, people understood the language of flowers. Each flower represented a human emotion. Shakespeare uses these symbols to express Ophelia's feelings as she walks to the stream, clutching garlands of nettles and daisies representing pain and innocence. Millais added more flowers, including violets around her neck to show faithfulness and pansies in the water to suggest love lost. What other flowers can you see?

WHY DON'T YOU?

Illustrate a scene from a book or play. Let your imagination go wild! If you pick a fantasy or science-fiction story, you can include spaceships, robots, aliens, dragons, dinosaurs, wizards....

✳ look at this

Can you find this robin in the main picture? It is hiding in the branches of the willow tree. In *Hamlet*, one of the songs Ophelia sings as she walks towards the stream includes the line, 'For bonny sweet Robin is all my joy.' Millais has included the robin to evoke this line from the play.

✳ Compare this

This was the first painting to be exhibited with the initials of the Pre-Raphaelite Brotherhood – PRB – on it. Can you find them? Based on 'Isabella', a poem by John Keats, the painting was also the work in which Millais introduced his new detailed style of painting that led to *Ophelia*. Millais used friends and fellow artists as the models for this painting of thirteen people eating together. Each face seems very real and expressive. Just like real people, his characters all show different characteristics and emotions.

People are already crowding round it. He can see the critic from *The Times* newspaper, but there is no sign yet of John Ruskin.

The subject of Millais's painting is Ophelia, a character in Shakespeare's play *Hamlet*. Shakespearian themes are popular with painters, but until now nobody has been brave enough to tackle Ophelia's death. Driven mad by sorrow, Hamlet's grief-stricken lover falls into a stream while trying to decorate the trees on the bank with flower garlands. Millais has chosen to show her floating in the water, surrounded by flowers, shortly before she drowns.

Millais spent ages tramping through the fields of Surrey with Hunt, trying to find the right spot to paint the background. Eventually he set up his easel and stool on the bank of the river Hogsmill near Ewell. He worked up to eleven hours a day all last summer, painting every leaf, reed and flower he could see, carefully leaving a space in the centre of the painting to add the central figure once he was back in London.

The following winter, Millais painted in the figure of Ophelia, paying nineteen-year-old Elizabeth Siddal to pose for him at his studio in Gower Street. His model wore an antique dress and lay in a bath full of water. He had tried to keep the water warm by lighting oil lamps underneath the tub, but one day he was so hard at work that he didn't realize they had gone out and she nearly froze to death. He got into a lot of trouble with her father for that.

Millais has also been in trouble just for being in the Pre-Raphaelite Brotherhood. At first he and his friends had kept the Brotherhood a secret, the only clue to its existence being the initials 'PRB' that they added to their paintings. Millais was the first to do this in 1849 with his painting *Lorenzo and Isabella*. But within a year the truth came out and the art critics were angry, believing the young artists were trying to overthrow the establishment. Now things are starting to calm down and their work is being praised again. Millais hopes this painting will be well received. Financially it has already been a success – an art dealer bought it for 300 guineas six months ago, before the paint was even dry.

Millais hears a voice he recognizes and turns around. John Ruskin has arrived with his wife Effie. Millais walks over to *Ophelia* with them. Ruskin looks at the painting for a long time. Millais feels nervous, but Effie smiles at him and that calms him a little. Ruskin asks where he painted the riverbank, saying it doesn't really look wild enough, and adds that Ophelia's face looks mottled and transparent. Millais feels deflated, but Ruskin hasn't finished. 'As for how you have painted *Ophelia*,' he continues, 'there is only one word for it.' Effie smiles again. 'Exquisite,' Ruskin says. 'Just exquisite.' Millais feels his heart skip a beat.

Self-portrait by John Everett Millais, aged 54

✳ Compare this

Millais painted this much later in his career, and has not paid quite as much attention to detail as he did when he was younger. Compare the leafy bank of *Ophelia* to the beach and sea here. The boys are listening to a sailor tell stories. One of the boys represents Walter Raleigh, who grew up to be a famous explorer – the toy boat hints at his future. Millais always liked painting stories, whether based on plays and poems (like *Ophelia* and *Lorenzo and Isabella*) or simply invented (as here).

WANT TO SEE MORE?

www.tate.org.uk/ophelia
http://smarthistory.org/pre-raphaelites-millais-ophelia.html
www.anglik.net/millais.htm

LA LOGE
Pierre-Auguste Renoir

Pierre-Auguste Renoir (1841–1919) was one of the leading Impressionist painters, and *La Loge*, painted in 1874, was shown in the first Impressionist exhibition in Paris. Rejecting the formal, academic style of painting favoured by the art establishment, Impressionist painters used vibrant dabs and strokes of colour to create an effect, or 'impression' of light.

La Loge shows a young woman and man seated in a box at the theatre. In Paris at this time most theatre seats were in private boxes where the woman would sit at the front and the man behind. The woman had a better view of the play but was also on display, as the bright house lights were not dimmed during the performance. The man, seated behind, could hide in the shadows and use his opera glasses to look at other people in the audience.

1874

Pierre-Auguste Renoir is still cold, despite all the rushing around he has been doing. He has been setting up borrowed gas lamps and trying to clear a space to pose two models. He is going to turn a corner of his new studio into a box at the theatre (*loge* in French) for his latest painting, *La Loge*.

Renoir pulls his coat around his thin body and stamps his feet. He starts lighting the gas lamps and hopes they will warm the studio up a little. He only moved to this location in Rue Saint-Georges in Paris, France, recently. It is bigger than his old studio on the Left Bank of the river Seine, and he likes being close to the Louvre. He is also close to the Opéra, a huge new theatre being built by Charles Garnier. It has been under construction for over ten years, but it still isn't finished. Theatres seem to be opening all over the place at the moment, Renoir thinks. Just a few weeks ago he was at the Italiens, a fashionable theatre with plush crimson curtains and gilded boxes. It gave him the idea to create a painting based on a couple in a theatre box, something no one has ever painted before.

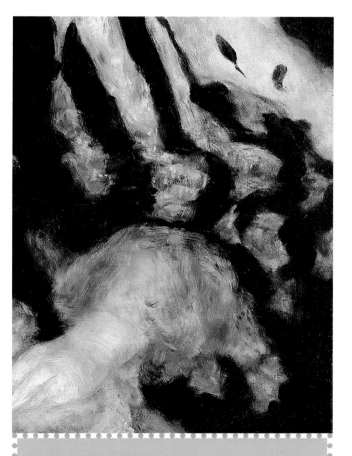

✳ look at this

From a distance the pink roses Renoir added to Nini's hair and dress are clearly flowers, but when you look closely they become abstract smudges of colour. He has used bold brushstrokes to paint them and used a wide range of colours – blue, green, white, red and pink. Despite this they appear as delicate blooms set off by her dark wavy hair. Ladies often wore fresh flowers in their hair at the theatre, but to keep them alive they had to place the flowers in slim glass vases of water that were then pinned into their hair. Let's hope they didn't leak!

✳ look at this

Look at the colour Renoir has added to the woman's sleeve and the man's white shirt-front to suggest they are in shadow. He has not used traditional browns or greys, but vivid blue. By using blue he allows us to see how the light creates shadows, but doesn't allow these shadows to appear dull or lifeless. Place an object near a light bulb and look at its shadow. What colours do you see?

DID YOU KNOW?

✳ When Renoir got old, he suffered from terrible arthritis. He could no longer hold a brush, so he would have one strapped on to his arm whenever he wanted to paint.

Self-portrait by Pierre-Auguste Renoir, c. 1875

Renoir has persuaded his younger brother Edmond, a writer and art critic, to pose as the man in the box and has paid a model, Nini Lopez, to pose as the woman. She is now getting changed behind a screen in the studio. Renoir has borrowed a fashionable black-and-white striped gown for her to wear, and has some fresh roses to add to her hair and dress. He also gives her a pair of white silk gloves.

He is anxious to get started. He wants the painting to be ready for the first Impressionist exhibition, which is due to open in a month's time. Renoir and his Impressionist friends have caused a stir in the art world by shunning the official Salon exhibition and deciding to put on their own show instead. Renoir still has doubts about whether they are doing the right thing. And he is worried about the sixty francs they are each having to put in to pay for the exhibition.

Nini now comes out from behind the screen. Renoir coils a long pearl necklace around her neck and fastens a gold bracelet on her right wrist. She smiles and says it is as if she is really going to the theatre. She has rubbed pearl-white make-up into her face to make it paler, and pinned her hair up. Now she tucks the roses into it and twirls around. Renoir is pleased. He thinks she looks perfect.

Edmond bursts through the door in his black trousers and coat, stiffened white shirt and cravat. He changed in his own apartment

✳ Compare this

Renoir painted this seven years after *La Loge*. It shows a group of friends eating outside at a restaurant overlooking the Seine on an island near Paris. As with *La Loge*, Renoir painted people from life, adding them to the canvas when they were able to sit for him. The artist Gustave Caillebotte sits backwards on a chair in a straw hat and vest, and the woman on the left with the dog is Renoir's future wife Aline Charigot. The restaurant owner stands with his daughter by the railing, and other friends who were hypnotists, journalists and actresses also posed for him.

WHY DON'T YOU?

Make an Impressionist masterpiece. If you have a computer with imaging software, you can use the Oil Painting tool in the Effects menu to help you.

downstairs and has worn the gold cufflinks that Renoir asked him to. He pulls on his cream kid leather gloves as he and Nini sit down on the chairs that Renoir has arranged. Renoir moves the gas lamps to ensure Nini's face is well lit and that Edmond is in shadow. The lamplight shimmers on Nini's necklace and the white silk gauze of her dress.

They have to sit still for some time as Renoir starts to work on the painting, using rapid feathery brushstrokes to suggest the light playing over their clothes and faces. He asks Nini to hold a pair of opera glasses in one hand, and a fan and handkerchief in the other. She starts to look through the glasses but Renoir says not to. He tells Edmond to look through his, though. 'Men do the looking at the theatre,' he says. 'Women are dressed up to be looked at.' Nini rolls her eyes. Edmond asks if he should look down, as if he is looking at the stage. 'No,' Renoir tells him. 'Look up, as if you are looking around the audience for people you know.'

Nini's hair keeps falling in her eyes and she is tired by the time Renoir says they can stop for the day. He wants them to come back tomorrow, but now he needs to eat. He sets off for the Café Guerbois, where he often meets fellow Impressionists Claude Monet and Alfred Sisley, his friends from student days. Today he can also see the painters Camille Pissarro and Edgar Degas there, and the photographer Félix Nadar. He sits down, as Pissarro and Monet start to discuss the final preparations for the exhibition, which will be held at Nadar's studio. Renoir hopes it is a success.

WANT TO SEE MORE?

www.courtauld.ac.uk/gallery/exhibitions/ 2008/renoir/details.shtml
www.courtauld.ac.uk/gallery/vodcasts/ renoir/02.shtml

✳ Compare this

In *The Umbrellas* Renoir painted the people on the right five years before he painted the people on the left. The little girl with the hoop, her mother and elder sister are all painted in his earlier style of soft feathery brushstrokes (the woman in *La Loge* is painted in a similar way). But the young woman with the basket on the left looks different. During the years he spent working on this painting, he decided to use stronger lines and blocks of colour. Do you think he painted the umbrellas at the same time as the girl with the hoop or the woman with the basket? How about the trees behind?

BREEZING UP (A FAIR WIND)
Winslow Homer

Winslow Homer (1836–1910) was one of the greatest American artists of the nineteenth century. He taught himself to paint while working as a commercial illustrator, drawing pictures for magazines. *Breezing Up (A Fair Wind)*, his most famous work, helped give him the confidence to concentrate on his painting full-time.

Breezing Up shows three boys and a man sailing in a strong breeze in their small catboat, *Gloucester*. Can you see the name written on the stern of the boat? The boy at the tiller is aiming the boat at a distant lighthouse, a landmark that will lead them safely back to harbour. The spray at the prow shows that the boat is flying along. Homer always signed his work. Can you find his signature?

DID YOU KNOW?

✱ Homer had no formal art training and taught himself to draw, encouraged by his mother, who was herself a talented amateur painter of birds and flowers.

✱ From childhood, Homer had been fascinated by the sea, and loved fishing and sailing.

✱ During the American Civil War, the magazine *Harper's Weekly* sent Homer to the battlefront as an artist-correspondent – a dangerous job!

1876

Winslow Homer has arranged to meet his older brother Charles, but he is running late. It took him longer than he thought to choose which suit to wear and to find his straw hat. Now he crosses the road into Madison Square and heads through the trees towards the National Academy of Design. The busy port of New York, on the eastern coast of America, is a bustling city, and with all the new hotels in the area there are lots of people to dodge as he hurries along.

Homer is going to meet his brother at the National Academy's annual exhibition, where his latest painting, *Breezing Up*, is on display. He exhibited his first proper painting – a scene of life in a Civil War army camp called *Home, Sweet Home* – at the annual exhibition thirteen years earlier. At the time Homer had been working as a commercial illustrator, copying photographs to be turned into prints for magazines such as *Harper's Weekly*. But a few years later he moved to New York to try and make a career as a painter. He is now a full member of the National Academy, and has finally given up doing illustrations so he can concentrate on painting full-time.

✳ look at this

These boys are enjoying their boat ride. The sun is on their backs, while the strong breeze fills the sail and propels the boat along. The boat has keeled over and both boys lean against the high edge to help balance the craft and stop it tipping over and sending them for an unexpected swim!

✳ look at this

Homer has called the boat 'Gloucester' because that is where his preparatory watercolours were painted. Look at the white spray over the rudder. Early on in his career Homer learned to use white paint to suggest the sun hitting surfaces. Here you can see it not only on the water, but also on the metal bar and the ring through which the rope controlling the sail is threaded.

WHY DON'T YOU?

Make friends with an artist! Find out all you can about your favourite painter – where they lived, what their family was like, what their hobbies were. Visit their paintings in a gallery, or look for images of their work on the internet. You might even like to try writing their life story. Lots of artists led quite dramatic lives!

Photograph of
Winslow Homer, aged 44

Breezing Up is based on Homer's watercolour studies of catboats, the single-masted sailing boats used in New England for fishing. Three years earlier, when he had started to experiment with watercolours, he had stayed in the fishing town of Gloucester, Massachusetts, and painted lots of seascapes and pictures of boys sailing. He had first tried watercolours as a child because his mother used them for her delicate paintings of birds. She'd made them look so easy to use, but he had found them hard to control. Now he loved the way they dried quickly and the bright colours he could achieve with them.

Homer decided to crew the boat in his painting with three boys and one man. The man sits next to the day's catch of fish, his hand tight on the sheet (rope) that controls the sail. But it's one of the boys who steers the boat towards the distant lighthouse, pulling on the rope attached to the rudder. All the boys sit on the same side of the boat to make sure it doesn't capsize. It's a windy day, and the full sail speeds them through the water, throwing up lots of spray.

Homer likes his paintings to look realistic, and he's very good at including accurate details to convince people his scenes are true to life. He has rigged the boat correctly, and he made lots of watercolour

✳ Compare this

In contrast to the choppy ocean in *Breezing Up,* this is a still lake where a boy is fishing. Look how differently Homer has painted the water. The picture is a watercolour, so instead of using white paint to show where the sun hits the water, Homer has left part of the paper blank. Homer loved fishing and solitude. Do you think he wants to be the boy in the boat? That might be why he accidentally signed this watercolour twice. Can you find both signatures?

studies of waves and skies before he started on the final painting. But he has also planned this composition carefully. The boys seem to be in charge of where this boat is going, and he has included another boat, a twin-masted schooner, on the horizon to show that soon the boys may be working on boats full-time, as sailors or fishermen. America was trying to rebuild itself after the recent Civil War, and everyone was talking about how the future of the country lay with its children.

Breezing Up is on sale in the exhibition for $850. While the positive response to it has given Homer confidence, it has been the regular sales of his watercolours that mean he's finally been able to give up illustration. His father hadn't been terribly clever with money and Homer had needed to be financially independent from a young age. Illustration had provided him with a steady income, but when he started painting he soon found he could produce watercolours quickly and sell them for $50 each. Their relatively low price means more people can afford his art, and so he sells lots of pictures. And he enjoys painting his scenes of the sea and boats, of boys fishing and playing together. He specially likes painting children – their games remind him of his youth growing up near Boston and playing in the nearby countryside.

Homer arrives at the National Academy and climbs the steps to the front door. His brother is waiting in the entrance, and after Homer has apologized for being late they walk through to see his paintings. In the past some critics have said that Homer's work was lazy and showed that he hadn't been to art school. But *Breezing Up* has silenced them – everybody likes it. Even today there's a small crowd around it. He hopes they can feel the wind in the boys' faces and smell the salt spray, and yearn – as he does – to be out there on the sea, in those perfect conditions, with a full catch in the boat.

✳ Compare this

Homer exhibited this picture at the National Academy of Design in 1863, during the American Civil War. Set in a Union camp, it is called *Home, Sweet Home*, the title of a popular song that the band in the background is playing. The music makes the two soldiers, one of whom has received a letter, think of how far away they are from their homes and how much they miss their loved ones. Homer's interest in colour theory is clear in the way he places red objects near green ones throughout the painting, making the colours seem more intense. How many red things can you see? Now look at *Breezing Up*, where he uses the same technique to make the green sea appear more striking by painting the man's top red.

WANT TO SEE MORE?

www.nga.gov/kids/homerscoop.pdf
www.nga.gov/feature/homer
www.artic.edu/aic/collections/exhibitions/
homer/behindscenes

SUMMER'S DAY
Berthe Morisot

Berthe Morisot (1841–1895) was among the leading Impressionist painters working in Paris in the late nineteenth century. *Summer's Day* is one of her best-known works, and shows her love of painting outdoors and of capturing the play of light across different surfaces.

This picture shows two young women sitting in a boat on the lake in the Bois de Boulogne, a fashionable park on the outskirts of Paris near Morisot's home. She first painted this scene with watercolours and then later copied it using oil paints. It is full of movement. Look at the rippling water, the swimming ducks, and the blurry horse and carriage on the far bank.

DID YOU KNOW?

✴ Morisot's brother-in-law, the painter Édouard Manet, encouraged her to paint, and once gave her an easel as a Christmas present.

✴ She liked to use her family and friends as models. Her daughter Julie was her favourite subject.

✴ She played the piano so well that the famous Italian composer Gioachino Rossini, who lived nearby, chose a new piano for her and signed it.

1879

Soft April sunlight falls across the piano in Berthe Morisot's drawing room on the fashionable Avenue d'Eylau. She lives in Passy, a village on the outskirts of Paris, France, with her husband Eugène Manet. She met him through his brother, the famous painter Édouard Manet. Édouard painted Morisot many times before her marriage to his brother, and they inspired each other to try out new ideas in their paintings. Morisot now has an eighteen-month-old daughter, Julie, who has just gone to sleep after a long walk in the nearby park, the Bois de Boulogne.

Morisot is seated by the window, reading the French newspaper *Le Temps*. Her dark eyes widen as she reads a review of the fifth Impressionist exhibition, in which she has exhibited fourteen paintings. She has shown work in all but one of the Impressionist exhibitions, and is regarded as a leading exponent of this new, loose and exciting painting style.

She finishes reading the review and mutters to herself. Her husband looks up from his paper enquiringly, and she tells him that the critic who wrote it has called her an 'unrepentant Impressionist'. Eugène Manet smiles, and says the critic is right. She is unrepentant in the way she tries to capture how light falls on people and places, and how it changes their appearance every second of every day. Along with Renoir and Claude Monet, Morisot has helped to pioneer this style of painting. The critic in the paper Manet is reading, *La Justice*, is more flattering. He writes of being seduced and charmed by Morisot's paintings, and says that *The Lake in the Bois de Boulogne* (now called *Summer's Day*) is painted 'with extraordinarily subtle tones'.

Morisot thinks about this painting, now in the exhibition being held in an unfinished building near the Louvre. She had been forced to stop work while she was pregnant, but last summer she completed several paintings set in the Bois de Boulogne. In this one, depicting two women in a boat on the lake, she has tried to capture the sunlight playing on the water. Morisot paid the two women to pose for her so she could paint them outdoors. It was quite hard for a middle-class woman like her to paint outside, as some places were considered out of bounds for women on their own. Painting in parks was acceptable, as they

✳ look at this

Look at the type of brushstrokes Morisot used to paint this picture. She uses zigzags all over the canvas to suggest the light falling on different surfaces, making them sparkle and shimmer. In close-up, these marks appear almost abstract, but when you look at the painting as a whole, they make it seem alive. Morisot's energetic style makes the scene pulse with life.

Portrait of Berthe Morisot, aged 31, by her future brother-in-law Édouard Manet

WANT TO SEE MORE?

www.arthistoryarchive.com/arthistory/
impressionism/Berthe-Morisot.html
www.renoirinc.com/biography/artists/
morisotlg.htm

✳ compare this

Morisot used professional models in many of her paintings, such as *Young Woman Dressed for the Ball*. This young woman looks quite like the one in *Summer's Day*. Do you think she is the same person? Both women in the paintings seem uneasy at being on show. This picture shows a young woman dressed for a party. The background has been painted quickly, using broad brushstrokes to give it energy.

were full of women and children. Morisot was pleased about this as it allowed her to work outside, something she had learned under one of her early teachers, the landscape painter Jean-Baptiste-Camille Corot.

Although Morisot loves painting in the Bois de Boulogne, she sometimes has to be content with painting indoors at home. She has sketched many portraits of Julie since she was born, and has also completed some larger paintings of women going to parties and balls. Her *Young Woman Dressed for the Ball* is also hanging in the exhibition, and has already sold.

Morisot is very pleased with *Summer's Day*. She painted it in response to Édouard Manet's painting *Boating*, which she had seen in his studio a few years earlier. But while his man and woman looked bored and lonely, her two women are set in a landscape that fizzes with life. Often Morisot feels depressed and unsure of herself, but as she thinks about this painting she feels her confidence returning. Yes, she thinks, she is an 'unrepentant Impressionist' and she is proud to be one.

WHY DON'T YOU?

Make a soundtrack for your favourite pictures. Many artists, such as Berthe Morisot and Angelica Kauffman, also liked to play and listen to music. Listen out for pieces of music that give you the same feeling as your favourite works of art. What kind of music would fit with Summer's Day?

✳ Compare this

This was painted two years after *Summer's Day* and shows Morisot's husband Eugène in the garden with their three-year-old daughter Julie. It illustrates Morisot's continued interest in trying to capture the effect of sunlight on objects. Look at the way she paints Eugène's brown jacket and Julie's pink coat – in places they are nearly white to suggest reflected light. Morisot did the same thing when she painted the lilac dress of the woman in the boat in *Summer's Day*, adding white highlights to her chest, arm and lap.

A SUNDAY ON LA GRANDE JATTE
Georges Seurat

Georges Seurat (1859–1891) was twenty-six when he finished his masterpiece *A Sunday on La Grande Jatte*. Its daring new style, called 'Neo-Impressionism', shocked some and inspired others. Seurat wanted to create harmonic, timeless scenes and used the latest scientific thinking and colour theory to help him do so.

Seurat wanted this work to be taken seriously, which is why he painted it on the same scale as the history paintings that filled the Salon, the official art exhibition, each year. But instead of illustrating a scene from history, it shows contemporary life. This shocked people, as they weren't used to seeing an artist give so much attention to everyday subjects.

DID YOU KNOW?

✳ When Seurat started out as an artist, he worked only in black and white for two years in order to understand tone (light and dark).

✳ Another artist, Edgar Degas, nicknamed Seurat 'the notary' (a type of lawyer), because he always dressed so neatly.

✳ Seurat's masterpiece includes one monkey, three dogs, eight boats and forty-eight people!

1886

A tall, handsome young man with a pointed beard and dark wavy hair is struggling to hold on to one end of a large canvas. It is June in Paris, France, and he is getting hot. The man is 26-year-old Georges Seurat, who has come to collect his painting *A Sunday on La Grande Jatte* from the eighth Impressionist exhibition, which has just ended. Another painter, Camille Pissarro, is helping Seurat as he tries to carry the painting down the stairs, through the smart café Maison Dorée, and on to the street.

Pissarro had helped Seurat get selected for the exhibition. He'd had to argue with the couple organizing the show, the painter Berthe Morisot and her husband Eugène Manet, who didn't think Seurat's bold new style had a place alongside Impressionist paintings. But Pissarro persuaded them in the end, even though it meant his own paintings would be tucked away with Seurat's in a separate room. Nonetheless, Seurat's painting became the talk of the show. In an article in *La Vogue*,

✳ look at this

The many-coloured dots Seurat used can be clearly seen on the man playing the trumpet. Look at his blue hat – not all the colours you can see are ones you would expect to find! Behind him two women sit on the grass in the shade of a tree, while two soldiers in uniform stand in the full sun. One critic said this painting wasn't very good because all the figures looked like toy soldiers – meaning they didn't look lifelike or real.

✳ look at this

Seurat painted a frame around the edge of the whole scene. Here it is made up mostly of red dots to contrast with the green grass. Because red and green are complementary colours they look brighter when they are next to each other. Orange and blue are also complementary colours – notice how the frame changes to blue when it is next to a patch of orange earth.

Photograph of
Georges Seurat, aged 29

the young art critic Félix Fénéon singled it out for repeated praise and said it represented an entirely new way of painting, which he called 'Neo-Impressionism'. Pissarro himself had already started to paint in this new style, as had another of Seurat's friends, Paul Signac.

Neo-Impressionism, also known as 'pointillism' or 'divisionism', was based on theories developed by scientists who had analyzed light. One of these scientists, Michel-Eugène Chevreul, had designed a colour wheel showing pairs of complementary colours, such as red and green and orange and blue. He had discovered that when these colours are placed next to each other they appear brighter than when placed apart. Another scientist, Ogden Rood, believed that colours mixed by an artist on a palette could seem duller than the same colours mixed in the eye.

In his earlier paintings, such as *Bathers at Asnières*, Seurat had mixed many of his colours. But in *A Sunday on La Grande Jatte* he experimented with these new theories, painting thousands of dots of different contrasting colours and hoping the viewer's eyes would mix them into the finished colours as they looked at the painting. Fénéon said the dots made the surface of the painting seem to tremble and come alive.

This technique is very time-consuming, and it has taken Seurat two years to finish this painting. To start with, he made lots of sketches on La Grande Jatte, an island in the river Seine near Paris. The painting is

✳ Compare this

A Sunday on La Grande Jatte was Seurat's second large-scale painting of contemporary life. His first was *Bathers at Asnières*, which shows factory workers relaxing on the banks of the river Seine. The island of La Grande Jatte can be seen across the water, and the factory where they work is visible beyond the railway bridge. Seurat experimented with complementary colour theory in this painting, but had not yet perfected his pointillist technique.

* compare this

Unlike *A Sunday on La Grande Jatte*, *The Circus* seems full of movement. As well as colour theory, Seurat studied the theory of lines and found that lines travelling upwards made the viewer feel happy. How many upward lines can you find? (Look at the dancer's arms and the clown's hair.) Now look at *A Sunday on La Grande Jatte*, with its static composition. How does that painting make you feel by comparison?

WHY DON'T YOU?

Make a pointillist picture using dots of colour. A good way to make dots is to dip the eraser ends of pencils into paint, then blot them on to your board or paper. Try using complementary colours next to each other, then look at your painting from a distance to see the effect this creates.

set in the park at one end of the island, and shows lots of different types of people enjoying themselves on a Sunday afternoon. But even though there are nearly fifty people in the scene, nobody seems to be talking to anyone else – in Seurat's eyes, this is modern life.

Once he had worked out where he was going to place all the figures, Seurat started painting, first in broad bands of colour and then with countless dots. It is not surprising it took him so long to finish – the canvas was so big that he had to use a stepladder to reach the top.

Paul Signac arrives at the exhibition just in time to open the door for Seurat and Pissarro. None of them knows it yet, but this will be the last Impressionist exhibition. Seurat and Signac's new style will grow in popularity, and Neo-Impressionism will take centre stage. But Seurat just wants to be back in his studio. He doesn't like crowds or parties, and is looking forward to some peace and quiet so he can plan his next painting with scientific precision.

WANT TO SEE MORE?

www.georgesseurat.org
www.artic.edu/aic/exhibitions/seurat/seurat_themes.html
www.webexhibits.org/colorart/jatte.html

MONT SAINTE-VICTOIRE
Paul Cézanne

Paul Cézanne (1839–1906) is often called 'the father of modern art'. He lived in isolation for much of his life, but later became increasingly influential – his paintings inspired many twentieth-century artists, such as Pablo Picasso and Henri Matisse. Cézanne created over sixty paintings of Mont Sainte-Victoire, a mountain near his home in Aix-en-Provence in the south of France.

This painting is from the first series of paintings of Mont Sainte-Victoire that Cézanne worked on between 1882 and 1890. It is one of the few he signed. He exhibited it in Aix-en-Provence eight years after completing it and most people didn't understand it or like it. But a young poet, Joachim Gasquet, kept telling Cézanne how great he thought it was, so Cézanne signed it and gave it to him.

1887

It is a warm summer's morning and Paul Cézanne is walking through the fields near his home. The sun has almost cleared the top of the nearby mountain and he picks up his pace. He wants to get to his sister's farm as soon as he can so he can resume his painting. He has been camped out there, in the shade of some pine trees, for two months now, walking to and from home each day carrying his easel, paints, canvas and brushes on his back. He has a broad-brimmed hat to keep the sun out of his eyes, and a long walking stick to clear his path. It's a fair way each day but he does it religiously, drawn to the mountain he has known his whole life, Mont Sainte-Victoire.

Cézanne is forty-eight, and in good health. His dark, bushy beard is making him hot, but he will soon reach the welcome cool of the pine trees where he can rest and unpack. He remembers a time when, as a

✳ look at this

Cézanne included a newly built railway viaduct in his painting, but this is not a picture of the modern world that his contemporaries Monet and Renoir wanted to depict. Cézanne's landscapes appear timeless. There are no roads or people and the houses are reduced to simple shapes between fields. The railway viaduct looks more like a Roman aqueduct. Cézanne's home town of Aix-en-Provence had been an important Roman city and he uses this feature to hint at the history of the area.

✳ look at this

When you study Cézanne's paintings close up, you see how carefully he applied each brushstroke, and how each patch of colour links to those around it. While this painting shows a landscape with a pine tree in the foreground and a mountain in the distance, it is also a flat painting made up of interlocking colours and shapes. The feathery branches fuse with the clouds and sky and bring the background and the foreground together. The greens and yellows of the fields blend with the pinks and blues of the mountain to create a harmonious whole.

WANT TO SEE MORE?

www.paul-cezanne.org
www.courtauld.ac.uk/gallery/vodcasts/
cezannes/02.shtml

✳ Compare this

Throughout his lifetime Cézanne was repeatedly drawn back to Mont Sainte-Victoire, and painted two large series of oil paintings based on this landscape. He also painted many watercolours of the mountain, including this one. It dates from the last few years of his life, when he had started his second series of paintings. Look at how differently this painting is constructed – much of the paper is left blank, a technique Cézanne started using to add highlights to his work.

*Self-portrait by
Paul Cézanne, aged 41*

child, he would run through these same fields on his way to swim in the river Arc. He would come with his schoolfriends, Paul Alexis and Émile Zola, and they would splash about together and dream of becoming poets.

Alexis and Zola are both writers now, living in Paris. Zola is a famous novelist, but last year he wrote a book about a failed artist that seemed to be based on Cézanne's own life, and Cézanne can't forgive him for that. Besides, he thinks, he isn't a failure – if the officials who run the annual Salon exhibition don't understand his work and keep rejecting his paintings, it's their loss. He wouldn't want all the fuss of Parisian life anyway. Cézanne's father has recently died, and the wealth he inherited means he doesn't have to sell his work to survive.

He heads uphill towards the farm, thinking of his childhood swims. He likes to paint people bathing, and has done several paintings on this theme in the past few years. But now his eye is turned once more on the mountain. He has already painted it quite a few times, but at each attempt he feels he still has more to learn from it.

Before Cézanne felt able to approach the mountain directly, he'd needed to build his confidence as a painter. To do this, he spent time working alongside the Impressionist Camille Pissarro, who'd helped to get his work included in the first Impressionist exhibition. But

Cézanne's vision is different from that of the Impressionists – while they aim to capture the ever-changing light, he prefers to distil the essence of his subject from repeated viewings.

Cézanne likes to build his paintings from parallel brushstrokes and patches of subtly different colours. He wants his landscapes to be timeless and classical, like those of Nicolas Poussin. He used to enjoy painting still lifes, constructed in his studio from fruit and plaster casts of sculptures, and sometimes he has painted people. But he needs over a hundred sittings to complete a portrait, and people have a habit of moving. So at the moment he prefers to stick to painting his favourite motif, the giant mountain that has been part of his life for so long.

He reaches the pine trees and removes his backpack, then sets up his easel in the exact spot he worked yesterday. Cézanne has been working on this painting for two months now, and it is coming along well. In some places he can still see the pale cream primed canvas and some of the dark blue brushstrokes with which he first sketched out the scene, but he thinks the painting is nearly finished. He selects a dark green oil paint from his palette and starts to work on the low branches of the pine tree in the foreground. He wants to make it seem as if the branches are part of the landscape behind them.

Cézanne wants everything to connect together on the surface. Paintings are flat objects, he thinks, and there's no reason to pretend otherwise. So he has curled the pine tree branches around the top of the mountain as if they are stroking it, pulling it forwards and shortening the thirteen kilometres (eight miles) between them. He has used similar patches of colour for the lower branches and the landscape beyond, so it is hard to work out where one stops and the other begins. But he has also tried to be faithful to the scene before him, and has included the railway viaduct at the foot of the mountain and the farm houses in the fields. Cézanne hopes that some day people will appreciate Mont Sainte-Victoire as much as he does.

✳ Compare this

As he grew older, Cézanne became more and more interested in what paint could do rather than the subject matter itself, and in this still life he plays visual games with the flatness of the painting. Look at the onion on the table – it seems as if its green shoots also belong to the still life painting propped against the studio wall, bringing the background and foreground together, just as the pine branches and sky connect in *Mont Sainte-Victoire*.

DID YOU KNOW?

✳ *Cézanne once refused to shake hands with the painter Édouard Manet because he said he hadn't washed for eight days and didn't want to get Manet dirty!*

✳ *Cézanne was passionately committed to art and, in a letter written a month before he died, swore to die 'with a paintbrush in my hand'.*

WHY DON'T YOU?

Make a landscape scene using strips of newspaper in different shades. You can make the edges jagged to suggest mountains, or flat for a seascape. Now cut a small foreground object – a figure, a tree – from the darkest paper and place it on the landscape. What happens when you make the foreground object bigger?

WHERE DO WE COME FROM?
WHAT ARE WE? WHERE ARE WE GOING?
Paul Gauguin

Paul Gauguin (1848–1903) taught himself to paint, and his bold, flat style influenced many artists. He travelled to the Pacific island of Tahiti looking for paradise, but in fact found life there very difficult. However, it was there he produced his greatest work, *Where Do We Come From? What Are We? Where Are We Going?*

This huge painting is four and a half metres long (fifteen feet) and shows the cycle of life, which can be read like a story from right to left. On the right is a baby, in the centre a young man picking a ripe mango and on the left an old woman. However, rather than telling a single story, Gauguin wanted his painting to be read like a poem, inspiring moods and feelings in the viewer.

DID YOU KNOW?

✳ As a teenager, Gauguin joined the French merchant navy and sailed around the world for six years.

✳ He once shared a studio with the painter Vincent van Gogh, but unfortunately the two artists didn't get along.

✳ Gauguin loved looking at art from around the world. He had photographs of Egyptian wall paintings, South American sculptures and Indonesian temple carvings.

1897

Paul Gauguin throws down his brush. The sun is setting, and soon the studio he has built himself will be dark. His feet ache and he hasn't eaten all day. He has no money for food or for the medicine he needs. He feels exhausted. But the giant painting he has been working on night and day throughout December is finally finished.

From the beginning, Gauguin has seen *Where Do We Come From? What Are We? Where Are We Going?* as his masterpiece. He doesn't think he will live much longer, and he wants to leave behind a work that sums up all his beliefs about what a painting could and should be. It is loosely based on his experience of life in Tahiti, the island in the Pacific Ocean he has called home for six years, but it has more in common with a dream or vision. It shows the cycle of human life from birth to death and is based on local people, as well as sculptures and paintings from around the world that Gauguin has seen in photographs. He painted it as if in a trance, and even he doesn't know what it all means — he had just felt an overwhelming urge to paint it. He'd had to use coarse sacking and thin paints because painting materials were so expensive for him, but now it is done.

✳ Look at this

Both top corners of the painting are yellow — Gauguin wanted the picture to look as if it were peeling off a wall, like an old fresco. On the left he wrote the title in French, and on the right he signed his name and drew a dog. The dog appears in some of his other paintings and seems to represent the artist himself.

✳ Look at this

Gauguin was attracted to art and objects from around the world, particularly from cultures very different to that of France. The old woman holding her head in her hands is based on a mummified body from Peru that Gauguin had seen in a photograph ten years earlier. His mother was from Peru, and Gauguin had spent six years of his childhood there.

WHY DON'T YOU?

Make your own gallery. Like Gauguin, you could collect pictures of objects from around the world. You could use postcards from museums, pictures cut from magazines or images downloaded from the internet. Mount them on a pinboard on the wall so you can change the display when you like. Why not try making themed 'exhibitions' on subjects such as animals, people or buildings?

Self-portrait by Paul Gauguin, aged 41

✳ Compare this

The Vision After the Sermon was finished nearly ten years before *Where Do We Come From?*, but both works show Gauguin's interest in painting a vision rather than reality. The women and their priest have just been to church, and imagine the Bible story of Jacob and the Angel has come to life in front of them. The red background is inspired by the medieval stained glass and Japanese prints that Gauguin liked. It makes the painting seem very flat and unrealistic.

Tahiti wasn't the first place that Gauguin had travelled to in an attempt to escape his old life. He had lived in the south of France with the Dutch painter Vincent van Gogh, in Panama as part of the workforce building the Panama Canal and in Brittany, northern France, with a group of artists including Émile Bernard. In Brittany, Gauguin had painted some pictures he was pleased with – including *The Vision After the Sermon* – but they didn't sell, and he was very poor. He had given up his large suburban house and his well-paid job in a stockbroker's office to become a painter, and when he couldn't pay the bills any more his wife Mette had taken their five children to her home country of Denmark.

Gauguin's friend Bernard had told him he should go to Tahiti to live simply and paint cheaply. Bernard had just read a novel about Tahiti that made it sound like paradise, and Gauguin read a guidebook that said the same. But when he arrived in the capital, Papeete, he realized the books hadn't told the truth. Tahiti was a French colony, and there were

WANT TO SEE MORE?

www.gauguingallery.com
www.abcgallery.com/G/gauguin/
gauguin.html
www.paul-gauguin.net

✱ compare this

Gauguin often painted local people during his time in Tahiti. In this painting two women sit on a yellow floor with the sea behind them. One is dressed in a traditional *parau* (skirt) and one in a shapeless pink dress of the kind brought to the island by French missionaries. But in *Where Do We Come From?* Gauguin painted most figures either naked or wearing simple loincloths. He wanted the painting to seem timeless, not connected to the contemporary world and its changing fashions.

lots of French people living there. Gauguin was horrified to find that Tahiti was just like France. Eventually he settled in Mataiea, forty kilometres (twenty-five miles) from Papeete, and built himself a hut.

But life in Tahiti was hard. Gauguin wasn't a fisherman or a hunter, so had to buy expensive tinned European food from Papeete. When the paintings he sent back to Paris finally sold, money was sent to him but it took months to arrive and was never enough. He was very ill, and suffered from depression. In the months before he started painting *Where Do We Come From?* he had been too sick to paint.

Now he lies down on his studio floor. The painting stretches along the whole of one wall, its bright yellows and oranges glowing in the fading light. He hasn't spent years planning this painting like that young chemist Seurat would have done, he thinks, and he isn't interested in painting light like the Impressionists. His painting has come from deep within him, a dream realized in paint. He has used every bit of energy he possessed to do it. He has nothing left to give, but has indeed created a masterpiece. How he has suffered for his art, he thinks, as he closes his eyes.

Chronologies of the Artists

Jan van Eyck

c. 1390 He is born in Maaseyck, a small town near Maastricht in Holland. He takes his name, van Eyck, from his home town.

1422 He works for John of Bavaria in The Hague in Holland. He is employed as his equerry and is the court painter.

1425 Following John of Bavaria's death, Van Eyck works for Philip the Good, Duke of Burgundy, and lives in Lille (now in France). He continues working as an equerry and court painter.

1426 His brother Hubert dies while painting *The Ghent Altarpiece*. Jan van Eyck completes it in 1432.

1428–29 He travels to Portugal to paint Princess Isabella of Portugal, Philip the Good's future wife.

1429 He moves to Bruges (now in Belgium) and continues to work for Philip the Good. He earns a substantial salary and Philip values him highly.

1432 He completes a preparatory drawing for a painting of Cardinal Albergati. It includes notes on colouring, and the painting based on it is very similar. This is his only surviving drawing.

1433 He marries Margaret and has several children. Philip the Good is godfather to one of them. Van Eyck paints his presumed self-portrait this year, *Portrait of a Man*.

1434 He completes **The Arnolfini Portrait**.

1435 He paints *The Madonna of Chancellor Rolin*.

1439 He paints his wife wearing a headdress similar to the one worn by Arnolfini's wife in *The Arnolfini Portrait*.

1441 Philip the Good pays him a salary until his death. He is buried at St Donatian's Cathedral in Bruges.

Paolo Uccello

c. 1397 He is born in Florence, Italy, to Dono di Paolo, a barber surgeon, and Antonia.

1407 In June, he enters Lorenzo Ghiberti's sculpture workshop as an apprentice and stays for eight years.

1412 He is promoted to assistant and starts to help Ghiberti with the early stages of his designs.

1415 He qualifies as a painter and joins the official painters' guild of Florence. This allows him to employ his own assistants but it is thought he never did, preferring to work alone. Nothing is known of the next ten years of his life.

1425 The government in Venice asks him to take charge of repairing the mosaics in the Basilica of San Marco, which were badly damaged in a fire. He is back in Florence by January 1431.

1432 He begins his earliest known paintings, two frescoes in the cloister of Santa Maria Novella church, and he starts to experiment with perspective.

1434 He buys a house on Via Della Scala, near Santa Maria Novella.

1435 Leon Battista Alberti publishes his influential guide to painting, *De Pictura*. Uccello starts work on his **Battle of San Romano** scenes.

1447 Uccello paints more frescoes for Santa Maria Novella, including *The Flood*.

1453 His wife Tommasa gives birth to Donato. Uccello is 56 when his son is born. His daughter Antonia arrives three years later. She becomes a painter.

1465 Uccello travels to Urbino with his son Donato to paint an altarpiece, but doesn't finish it.

1468 By November he is back in Florence and claims on his tax return that he can no longer work because he is old.

1475 He dies in Florence on 12 December, aged 78.

Sandro Botticelli

1445 He is born in Florence, the youngest of four children. Named Alessandro di Mariano di Vanni Filipepi, he is known as Sandro.

1458 As a teenager, he works for his brother Antonio, who is a goldsmith. The whole family live together in the Ognissanti quarter, a poor district of Florence, where their father works as a tanner (a person who turns animal skins into leather).

1464 Botticelli enters the workshop of the successful painter Filippo Lippi, who is working on a cycle of frescoes in Prato, just outside Florence.

1470 By this date Botticelli has his own workshop and is accepting commissions. Filippino, the son of Filippo Lippi, is now his assistant. Botticelli's workshop is at the house he shares with his entire family. He lives and works there his whole life.

1472 He becomes a member of the Florentine guild of painters.

1473 His reputation reaches Pisa and he is asked to paint a fresco for Pisa's cathedral (the commission is later cancelled).

1475 He paints *The Adoration of the Magi* for Santa Maria Novella in Florence, including himself in the crowd.

1477 He starts work on **Primavera** for Lorenzo di Pierfrancesco de'Medici. He has three assistants at this time and they are all kept busy, as Botticelli's work is much in demand.

1481 He is summoned to Rome to paint three frescoes for the Sistine Chapel at the Vatican. His father dies while he is in Rome and he returns to Florence in 1482.

1503 By this time his style of painting is thought to be old-fashioned and few people commission him anymore. He struggles to pay his membership fees to the painters' guild.

1510 He dies in May in Florence, at the age of 65.

Leonardo da Vinci

1452 He is born on 15 April in or near the village of Vinci, near Florence.

1469 He enters the studio of Andrea del Verrocchio in Florence as an apprentice after his father shows the successful painter his son's drawings.

1472 He qualifies as a master of the painters' guild of St Luke, after painting an angel in Verrocchio's *The Baptism of Christ*. This allows him to set up his own studio and work independently.

1474 He paints his first known female portrait, Ginevra de Benci, the daughter of a friend.

1482 After moving to Milan he works for Ludovico Sforza, the Duke of Milan.

1484–85 He becomes interested in town planning as Milan experiences severe outbreaks of the plague.

1493 He completes an eight-metre-high clay model of a horse to be cast in bronze for the Duke of Milan, but the sculpture is never made.

1499 He leaves Milan to escape French soldiers who have conquered the city. He travels to Mantua and Venice before returning to Florence in April 1500.

1501 He starts work on *The Madonna of the Yarnwinder*, which has a similar landscape background to the *Mona Lisa*.

1502–03 He works for Duke Cesare Borgia as a military engineer across northern Italy.

1503 He returns to Florence in March and begins the **Mona Lisa** and *The Battle of Anghiari*, as well as being involved in engineering projects.

1506 He moves back to Milan, with the *Mona Lisa*, and spends more and more time drawing anatomical studies.

1513 He moves to Rome looking for work but doesn't settle there.

1516 He moves to France and lives near the royal palace at Amboise after the King of France, Francis I, offers him a pension.

1519 He dies in France on 2 May, at the age of 67.

Pieter Bruegel the Elder

1527 He is born in Breda, now in the Netherlands.

c. 1545 He goes to work in the studio of Pieter Coecke van Aelst, a successful painter and publisher who works in Antwerp and Brussels.

1551 He becomes a master of the Antwerp painters' guild.

1552 He travels to Italy to study Italian art, as many artists did at that time. He works in the studio of the Croatian miniaturist Giulio Clovio in Rome, possibly painting landscapes for him. Although he stays several years, Italian art doesn't make much of an impression on his own painting style.

1555 He returns to Antwerp through the Alps and creates drawings of the mountainous landscapes he saw. These are published as prints by Hieronymus Cock's Four Winds publishing house. He completes forty drawings for Cock's engravers to turn into prints over the next eight years.

1559 He paints *Netherlandish Proverbs*. The following year he completes **Children's Games**.

1562 He visits Amsterdam.

1563 He marries Mayken Coecke, the daughter of his artist-mentor, and moves to Brussels.

1564 His son Pieter is born: he becomes an artist, known as Pieter Bruegel the Younger, and copies many of his father's peasant paintings for a new audience.

1565 Bruegel the Elder completes a series of pictures called 'The Months'. Only five of the paintings survive. *Hunters in the Snow* probably represents the month of January.

1568 His second son Jan is born: he also becomes a painter, chiefly of flowers and landscapes.

1569 Bruegel dies in Brussels on 9 September. His friend the map-maker Abraham Ortelius says he died in the prime of his life. He was only 42.

Diego Velázquez

1599 He is born Diego Rodríguez de Silva y Velázquez in Seville, southern Spain.

1610 Aged eleven he starts a six-year apprenticeship with the painter Francisco Pacheco, living and working with the artist.

1617 He qualifies as a master painter in Seville, and works there until 1622. He paints **An Old Woman Cooking Eggs** a year after he qualifies.

1618 He marries Juana Pacheco, the daughter of the painter he studied with. Velázquez is eighteen; Juana is fifteen. Their first daughter, Francisca, is born the following year.

1622 Velázquez visits Madrid to try and persuade King Philip IV of Spain to be painted by him, but he doesn't succeed. His second daughter, Ignacia, is born this year.

1623 The following year he journeys to Madrid again and this time paints the king. He is made a painter at the king's court and moves his family to Madrid. They never leave.

1628 He is promoted to chief court painter.

1629–31 He travels to Italy to study the work of Italian painters such as Titian and Michelangelo. While he is away, the king refuses to let anyone else paint him or his family.

1648 He travels to Italy again, this time as an ambassador for the king to buy paintings for his palace.

1652 He is appointed the king's chamberlain, the highest position at court.

1659 He becomes a Knight of the Order of Santiago.

1660 He falls ill with a fever. The king visits his bedside, but he dies in August.

Johannes Vermeer

1632 He is born in Delft in the Netherlands, baptized in the New Church on 31 October, and lives in the city his whole life.

1641 His father works as an inn-keeper and art dealer. He buys Mechelen, an inn on Market Place, with a large house attached. It is popular with artists and craftsmen and has lots of paintings on the walls.

1650 Several talented painters settle in Delft, and Vermeer may have trained in the studio of Carel Fabritius.

1652 Vermeer's father dies. Vermeer probably helps his mother run the inn. He also starts to trade in paintings.

1653 He marries Catharina Bolnes on 20 April against her mother's wishes. On 29 December he becomes a master of the painters' guild.

1654 An explosion in a gunpowder magazine (store) destroys much of the city and kills the painter Carel Fabritius. Vermeer is written about as Delft's greatest painter now. He is 22.

1656 His first child, Maria, is born.

1660 By December Vermeer and Catharina are living with Catharina's mother, Maria Thins, in her large house on the Oude Langedijck, not far from Market Place.

1661 Vermeer visits The Hague on business relating to an inheritance of Catharina's. Catherina and her mother's incomes are substantial but, with an eventual fifteen children to support, money is never plentiful.

1662–63 Vermeer becomes the governor of the painters' guild, and is reappointed from 1667 to 1671.

1672 He visits The Hague to be an expert witness in a dispute concerning a group of Italian paintings.

1675 He dies in Delft and is buried in the Old Church. Several months later his wife is declared bankrupt. Despite being in debt for many years, Vermeer never sold **The Art of Painting**.

Jean-Baptiste-Siméon Chardin

1699 He is born in Paris, France, on 2 November. His father is cabinet-maker to the King, and makes billiard tables. He wants his son to continue his trade but Chardin wants to be an artist.

1718–28 Pierre-Jacques Cazes and later Noël-Nicolas Coypel teach Chardin to draw and paint.

1723 Chardin becomes engaged to Marguerite Saintard on 6 May, though their wedding isn't held until 1731. They have two children before her death in 1735.

1724 Chardin becomes a master painter at the Académie de Saint-Luc.

1728 On 25 September, after exhibiting **The Skate** and other works at the Young Painters' Exhibition in Place Dauphine, he is voted a member of the Académie Royale.

1733 He paints his first figures in genre scenes. Before this, he only painted still lifes.

1737 Following the reopening of the Salon, the official annual art exhibition in Paris, he exhibits between one and nine paintings there every year.

1743 He becomes a council member of the Académie Royale.

1744 He marries Françoise Marguerite Pouget. In 1745 they have a daughter.

1752 Louis XV grants him a yearly allowance, and in 1757 lets him live in an apartment in the Louvre.

1754 His son Jean-Pierre wins first prize in painting at the Académie Royale, but doesn't turn his early promise into a successful career.

1755 Chardin becomes treasurer of the Académie Royale.

1756 He returns to painting still lifes.

1774 He resigns as treasurer but continues to attend meetings until a month before his death.

1779 He dies on 6 December at his apartment in the Louvre.

Angelica Kauffman

1741 She is born on 30 October in Chur, Switzerland, but grows up in Austria. Her father is an artist who often travels to find work.

1753 By the age of twelve, when the family move to Lake Como in Italy for a year, she is a child prodigy, painting portraits of important people.

1754 Her family go to Milan and she spends her time copying works of art.

1757 Her mother dies on 1 March, and she moves with her father to his home town of Schwarzenberg in Germany, where they decorate the local church before returning to Milan.

1760 They move to Florence.

1762 She is elected a member of the Florence Art Academy – a great honour because it is the oldest art academy in Italy, and she is not yet 21.

1763 She moves to Rome, then travels to Naples to paint tourists' portraits and start her first history paintings.

1764 She returns to Rome and paints portraits of wealthy Europeans on their Grand Tour. The next year she becomes a member of the Rome Art Academy, then travels to Venice.

1766 She moves to England and is soon in demand as a portrait artist.

1767 Her father joins her in London. She is married briefly to a man who claims to be a Count but is a fraud.

1768 She becomes a founder member of London's Royal Academy.

1781 She marries the Venetian artist Antonio Zucchi, and in July they move to Venice with her father.

1782 Her father dies and she is heartbroken. She goes to Rome, then Naples, painting portraits of aristocratic tourists.

1794 Back in Rome, she paints **Self-Portrait Hesitating Between the Arts of Music and Painting**.

1795 Her husband dies.

1807 She dies on 5 November of a fever.

Caspar David Friedrich

1774 He is born on 5 September in Greifswald (then part of Sweden).

1781 His mother Dorothea dies.

1787 Caspar and his younger brother Johann Christoffer are out ice-skating when the ice breaks and Johann drowns.

1788 Caspar studies drawing with Johann Gottfried Quistorp.

1791 Caspar's sister Maria dies.

1794–98 He studies drawing at the Copenhagen Academy, returning to Greifswald in May 1798. In October he moves to Dresden.

1799 He takes part in the Dresden Academy annual exhibition, showing only drawings until 1807.

1806 After an illness he returns to Greifswald, then spends time on the nearby island of Rügen. The following year he takes up oil painting.

1808 He paints The Tetschen Altar, his first major painting of a cross in a mountain landscape.

1809 His father dies. He paints **The Monk by the Sea** and its companion piece The Abbey in the Oak Wood. The following year the two paintings are exhibited and sold at the Berlin Art Academy. The year after, Friedrich is elected a member of the Academy.

1811 He goes on a walking tour of the Harz Mountains.

1815 He becomes a member of the Dresden Art Academy.

1818 On 21 January he marries Caroline Bommer.

1819 His daughter Emma is born. His second daughter Agnes arrives in 1823, the year he starts work on The Sea of Ice. His son Gustav is born in 1824, and Friedrich is made a professor at the Dresden Art Academy but falls ill.

1835 He has a stroke and his right hand stops functioning. A further stroke in 1837 leaves him almost completely paralysed.

1840 He dies on 7 May in Dresden.

Théodore Géricault

1791 He is born on 26 September in Rouen, France. His wealthy family support his dream of becoming an artist even though they don't see it as a good career for him.

1808 The artist Carle Vernet gives him a few painting lessons.

1810 He studies with the classical painter Pierre Guérin, but spends most of his time copying paintings in the Louvre, Paris.

1812 His first painting, The Charging Chasseur, is accepted into the Salon, the official art exhibition in Paris. It is a huge painting and wins the gold medal.

1814 His second painting, The Wounded Cuirassier (also huge), is criticized at the Salon.

1816 He spends the year in Italy studying the paintings of Renaissance masters such as Michelangelo and Raphael. The Medusa is shipwrecked off the coast of Africa on 2 July. Géricault decides to paint the raft, after two of the survivors publish their story.

1818 He moves out of his father's house in November and locks himself away in his studio for eight months to paint **The Raft of the Medusa**.

1819 The painting wins the gold medal at the Salon. Géricault is exhausted and spends time in the countryside outside Paris trying to recover.

1820 He is asked to exhibit the painting in England. Fifty thousand people pay to see it.

1821 He returns to France in December. The director of the Louvre tries to convince the government to buy the painting, but they ignore him.

1822 Géricault is seriously ill. The following year he is confined to bed. His spine is disintegrating, possibly because of tuberculosis.

1824 He dies on 26 January. He is 32 years old. The director of the Louvre finally scrapes together enough money from the government to buy The Raft of the Medusa.

John Constable

1776 He is born on 1 June in East Bergholt, a village in Suffolk, England. He is the fourth of six children, and they all grow up in a large house their father, a wealthy miller, built.

1795 After seeing Hagar and the Angel by Claude, owned by Sir George Beaumont, Constable realizes he wants to be a painter. His father wants him to become a vicar or enter the family business.

1799 He persuades his father to let him train as a painter at the Royal Academy in London.

1802 His first painting is included in the important summer exhibition at the Royal Academy.

1809 He falls in love with Maria Bicknell, but doesn't make enough money to marry her.

1816 His father dies and leaves him enough money to marry Maria. They live in London and have seven children.

1819 Constable exhibits his first 'six-footer', The White Horse, at the Royal Academy.

1821 **The Hay Wain** goes on show at the Royal Academy. During the summer Constable rents a house in Hampstead, overlooking London, and relentlessly paints and sketches the clouds.

1824 The Hay Wain is bought by a dealer who exhibits it in Paris at the Salon, the French equivalent to the Royal Academy summer exhibition. His work is highly praised by artists and King Charles X awards it a gold medal. Constable does not visit the Salon, and never travels to France.

1828 Maria dies of tuberculosis. Constable is heartbroken, and his paintings reflect his sadness with dark, stormy skies and isolated ruins.

1829 He finally becomes a full member of the Royal Academy, aged 52.

1837 He dies on 31 March and is buried next to Maria in Hampstead.

Gustave Courbet

1819 He is born Jean Désiré Gustave Courbet on 10 June in Ornans, France.

1837 His parents want him to study law, but instead he studies art in the nearby town of Besançon, following lessons from a local painter.

1839 He moves to Paris and studies with a minor painter while copying paintings in the Louvre.

1844 His first painting is accepted at the Salon. It is called *Self-Portrait with a Black Dog*.

1847 His son is born to Virginie Binet. Between 1841 and 1847 he submits twenty-five paintings to the Salon, but only three are accepted. He hardly sells anything for years and relies on his father, a wealthy farmer, sending him money to survive.

1849 He wins the gold medal at the Salon for *After Dinner at Ornans*. This allows him to exhibit at the Salon in future years without putting his work in front of a selection committee.

1850–51 *The Stone Breakers*, *Peasants of Flagey Returning from the Fair* and **A Burial at Ornans** are exhibited at the Salon.

1853 The government asks him to paint a large work for the forthcoming World Exhibition as long as he submits a sketch in advance. He refuses. Later he submits fourteen works, but three are rejected because they are too big.

1855 He holds his own exhibition to coincide with the World Exhibition, and shows *The Painter's Studio* alongside *A Burial at Ornans* in his 'Pavilion of Realism'. At this time no one has ever done such a thing. He travels more and more, and exhibits abroad.

1871 He is jailed and fined for the destruction of the Vendôme Column, a monument celebrating Napoleon.

1873 He is told he has to pay to replace the Column, which he cannot afford to do. He is forced into exile and moves to Switzerland.

1877 He dies in Switzerland on 31 December, aged 58.

John Everett Millais

1829 He is born on 8 June in Southampton, England, but grows up on the island of Jersey.

1838 The family move to London and rent a house near the British Museum so Millais can attend Henry Sass's Art Academy.

1840 At the age of eleven, he becomes the youngest ever student at the prestigious Royal Academy school. He studies there for six years.

1844 He meets William Holman Hunt.

1846 He joins a drawing club with Hunt and Dante Gabriel Rossetti. His first painting for the Royal Academy's summer exhibition is accepted.

1848 He forms the Pre-Raphaelite Brotherhood with Hunt, Rossetti and other friends.

1849 He exhibits *Lorenzo and Isabella* at the summer exhibition. No one knows what the initials PRB, included in the painting, mean.

1850 He exhibits *Christ in the House of his Parents (The Carpenter's Shop)* at the Royal Academy. It is not liked.

1851 The art critic John Ruskin publishes letters and essays supporting the group. He also starts to buy their work, particularly Millais's.

1852 Ophelia is exhibited at the Royal Academy.

1853 Millais paints Ruskin's wife in *The Order of Release*. They eventually marry. He becomes the youngest ever Associate of the Royal Academy.

1856 His son Everett is born, the first of eight children. Increasingly Millais becomes a portrait artist to support his family.

1863 He becomes an Academician, a full member of the Royal Academy.

1885 He is the first ever artist to receive a hereditary baronetcy, and becomes Sir John.

1896 He is appointed President of the Royal Academy, but dies on 13 August at the age of 67.

Pierre-Auguste Renoir

1841 He is born on 25 February in Limoges, France. His father is a tailor and his mother a dressmaker.

1844 The family move to Paris.

1854 Renoir is offered a place in the chorus of the Paris Opera, but he doesn't want to sing for a living. He becomes an apprentice at a porcelain factory, painting portraits on tea cups.

1862 He studies at Charles Gleyre's studio with Claude Monet, Alfred Sisley and Frédéric Bazille. They copy masterpieces in the Louvre as well as learn to paint outdoors.

1869 He and Monet paint the restaurant La Grenouillère on the banks of the Seine. They produce their first Impressionist-style paintings.

1870 On 19 July the Franco-Prussian war begins. Renoir joins the cavalry. His friend Bazille is killed.

1871 After the war, Monet introduces Renoir to the art dealer Paul Durand-Ruel, who sells some of his paintings. Renoir moves into a bigger studio.

1874 The first Impressionist exhibition opens in the photographer Nadar's studio in Paris. Renoir shows **La Loge**.

1879 He returns to exhibiting his paintings at the official Salon rather than with his friends the Impressionists. He shows a big portrait of Madame Charpentier and her daughters and is soon much in demand as a portrait artist.

1881 He tours around Algeria, Spain and Italy, looking at art.

1882 He marries Aline Charigot, a former model. They have three sons.

1897 He falls off his bicycle and breaks his arm. This leads to an ongoing problem with arthritis.

1903 He moves to the Riviera in the south of France, later building a house with a glass studio in the garden.

1919 He dies on 3 December after years spent in a wheelchair, crippled by arthritis but painting every day until he died.

Winslow Homer

1836 He is born on 24 February in Boston, Massachusetts, in America.

1842 His family move to Cambridge, Massachusetts, where his father opens a hardware store (he later goes to California to try and find gold, but fails to strike it rich).

1854 Homer starts work as a commercial illustrator. During his two-year apprenticeship for J. H. Bufford's in Boston he copies lithographs and photographs to be turned into new prints.

1857 He sets up on his own as a freelance illustrator, working mainly for the new journal *Harper's Weekly*.

1859 He moves to New York and enrols in life-drawing classes at the National Academy of Design.

1861 Frederick Rondel and Thomas Seir Cummings give him private lessons in oil painting. The American Civil War begins in April and for four years Homer paints little else.

1863 *Home, Sweet Home* is included in the National Academy of Design annual exhibition. It is the first time one of Homer's paintings is exhibited.

1866 In December he goes to France and spends nearly a year in Paris. He visits the 1867 Universal Exhibition, where two of his paintings are shown.

1873 He visits the fishing community of Gloucester, Massachusetts, and paints lots of watercolours.

1875 He becomes a full-time painter, and the following year **Breezing Up (A Fair Wind)** is exhibited.

1881 Homer sails to England, where he spends most of his time in a fishing village, painting dramatic sea rescues and local women.

1882 He returns to New York but decides to go and live by the sea.

1883 He moves to Prout's Neck, a fishing village near Portland in Maine. He lives there for the rest of his life.

1910 He dies in his studio on 29 September. He is 74.

Berthe Morisot

1841 She is born on 14 January in Bourges, France, and has two elder sisters Yves and Edma.

1845 Her younger brother Tiburce is born. They grow up in Passy on the outskirts of Paris. Berthe lives in Passy all her life.

1857 Edma and Berthe are taken for drawing lessons at the studio of Geoffroy-Alphonse Chocarne. They later study with Joseph Guichard, who takes them to draw at the Louvre.

1860 Berthe studies with Jean-Baptiste-Camille Corot.

1864 Edma and Berthe have their work accepted by the Salon.

1869 Edma marries, stops painting and moves to Brittany. Berthe begins to sit for portraits by Édouard Manet.

1874 She takes part in the first Impressionist exhibition, and shows *The Cradle*. In the winter she marries Manet's brother, Eugène.

1876 She shows nineteen works at the second Impressionist exhibition. The following year she also takes part in the third Impressionist exhibition.

1878 Her daughter Julie is born on 14 November.

1879 She doesn't exhibit in the fourth Impressionist exhibition, but continues to paint and completes **Summer's Day**.

1880 She takes part in the fifth Impressionist exhibition. The following year she also takes part in the sixth Impressionist exhibition.

1882 The family go to Nice but Julie becomes ill. Eugène returns to Paris and submits Berthe's paintings to the seventh Impressionist exhibition.

1886 She and Eugène organize the eighth and last Impressionist exhibition.

1891 Eugène dies.

1892 A solo show of Berthe's work, organized by Eugène before he died, opens in Paris.

1895 She dies on 28 February, aged 54.

Georges Seurat

1859 He is born Georges-Pierre Seurat in Paris on 2 December. He lives at 136, Boulevard Magenta, near the Gare du Nord, with his parents. His father is a civil servant and earns enough so that his son doesn't have to worry about money when he becomes a painter.

1878 He becomes a student at the Ecole des Beaux-Arts in Paris. His teacher is Henri Lehmann, a follower of the famous Neo-Classical painter Jean-Auguste-Dominique Ingres. Seurat walks out after little more than a year, as he is not a very attentive student.

1880 After completing his compulsory year of military service at the port of Brest in Brittany, where he sketched the ships, he returns to Paris. He rents a studio with student friends and begins to work again, concentrating on black-and-white drawings for two years.

1884 He finishes *Bathers at Asnières*, and starts to develop his new style, painting in thousands of coloured dots. In May he begins **A Sunday on La Grande Jatte**. The same year he meets artist Paul Signac and helps to launch the Société des Artistes Indépendants (Independent Artists Society).

1886 *A Sunday on La Grande Jatte* is exhibited at the eighth and final Impressionist exhibition in Paris. A young art critic, Félix Fénéon, champions Seurat and calls his new style 'Neo-Impressionism'.

1887 Seurat exhibits his work with the Belgium group The Twenty in Brussels, along with other guest artists including Paul Gauguin, Vincent van Gogh and Paul Signac.

1890 Seurat's girlfriend Madeleine Knobloch gives birth to his son, Pierre.

1891 He dies suddenly in Paris, aged 31, possibly of meningitis.

Paul Cézanne

1839 He is born on 19 January in Aix-en-Provence, southern France. His father is a hat retailer and banker.

1852 Cézanne starts secondary school and becomes friends with Émile Zola, later a famous novelist.

1858 Cézanne starts attending drawing classes, but his father tells him he has to study law.

1861 He gives up studying law and travels to Paris to try and enter the École des Beaux-Arts. He doesn't get in and is depressed. He returns to Aix to work in his father's bank.

1862 He goes back to Paris in November and studies at the Atelier Suisse. The following year he meets Monet, Degas and Renoir.

1860s He repeatedly fails to get his work selected for the Salon.

1870 During the Franco-Prussian War, he moves to L'Estaque near Marseilles with his girlfriend Hortense Fiquet, to avoid being made to fight.

1872 He has a son and calls him Paul. They move to Auvers-sur-Oise near Paris and he spends the following year painting alongside Camille Pissarro.

1874 *The House of the Hanged Man at Auvers-sur-Oise* is included in the first Impressionist exhibition.

1877 He has sixteen paintings in the third Impressionist exhibition.

1886 Zola publishes his novel *L'Œuvre* ('The Masterpiece'), about a failed artist. Cézanne refuses to see him any more. The same year Cézanne's father dies and leaves him a lot of money.

1887 He paints **Mont Sainte-Victoire**, a mountain near Aix. In all he paints it over sixty times.

1895 The art dealer Ambroise Vollard holds Cézanne's first one-man show.

1901 He buys a small country house north of Aix, where he builds a studio.

1906 He collapses during a storm while painting outdoors, and dies on 22 October. He is 67 years old.

Paul Gauguin

1848 He is born Eugène Henri Paul Gauguin on 7 June in Paris, France.

1849 His family sail to Peru. His father dies on the voyage and the family go to live with his mother's great-uncle.

1855 The family return to France and Gauguin grows up in Orléans, moving to Paris in 1862, where his mother works as a seamstress.

1865 He joins the French merchant navy and travels round the world. His mother dies in 1867 while he is at sea.

1871 He returns to Paris and works for a stockbroking firm.

1873 After marrying Mette, a young Danish woman, he starts painting in his spare time. His son Émile is born a year later, the first of five children.

1876 His first painting is accepted by the Salon. He resigns as a stockbroker a year after the 1882 stockmarket crash, and tries to support his family as a full-time painter.

1884 Mette insists they all go to Denmark, as Gauguin is too poor to support them. He returns to work in Paris a year later without them, sticking up railway posters for money and exhibiting with the Impressionists.

1886 He moves to Pont-Aven in Brittany and works alongside other artists, including Émile Bernard. He meets Vincent van Gogh in Paris and later travels to Arles to live and work with him, but it is not a success and he returns to Paris two months later.

1891 He decides to go to Tahiti, and stays until 1893. He returns to Paris to recover from illness but goes back to Tahiti in 1895.

1897 He is still unwell when he paints **Where Do We Come From? What Are We? Where Are We Going?**

1898 He tries to poison himself by swallowing arsenic, but ends up being violently sick instead and survives.

1903 He dies on the Marquesas Islands, 800 miles north of Tahiti, where he moved in 1901.

Museums to Visit

The Arnolfini Portrait

National Gallery, London, England: www.nationalgallery.org.uk

The Arnolfini Portrait travelled from Bruges to Holland, Hungary and Spain before it ended up in England. It was bought by the National Gallery in 1842 for £6,000.

The Battle of San Romano

National Gallery, London, England: www.nationalgallery.org.uk

The second panel of the triptych is in the Uffizi Gallery in Florence, Italy, and the third panel is in the Louvre in Paris, France.

Primavera

Galleria degli Uffizi, Florence, Italy: www.uffizi.com

The Uffizi Gallery has a whole room dedicated to Botticelli. It contains many famous works, including his Birth of Venus.

Mona Lisa

Musée du Louvre, Paris, France: www.louvre.fr

The Mona Lisa used to hang in Napoleon's bedroom, but now it hangs in its own room at the Louvre and millions of people visit it every year.

Children's Games

Kunsthistorisches Museum, Vienna, Austria: www.khm.at

The Kunsthistorisches Museum has the finest collection of Bruegel paintings in the world.

An Old Woman Cooking Eggs

National Gallery of Scotland, Edinburgh, Scotland: www.nationalgalleries.org

If you want to see Velázquez's portraits of the Spanish royal family, many can be found in the Museo del Prado in Madrid, Spain.

The Art of Painting

Kunsthistorisches Museum, Vienna, Austria: www.khm.at

This painting is known by several different titles, including The Artist's Studio.

The Skate

Musée du Louvre, Paris, France: www.louvre.fr

This painting is often called The Ray, or The Rayfish. Rays and skates are similar-looking fish, but experts now think the painting shows a skate.

Self-Portrait Hesitating Between the Arts of Music and Painting

Nostell Priory, West Yorkshire, England: www.nationaltrust.org.uk/main/w-nostellpriory

In this book the artist's name is written as 'Angelica Kauffman', but the spelling varies. Elsewhere you might see it as 'Angelika Kauffmann'!

The Monk by the Sea

Alte Nationalgalerie, Berlin, Germany: www.smb.spk-berlin.de

In the Alte Nationalgalerie, The Monk by the Sea hangs side by side with The Abbey in the Oak Wood, as the artist intended.

The Raft of the Medusa

Musée du Louvre, Paris, France: www.louvre.fr

When Géricault first sent this painting to the Salon, he suddenly realized it needed two more figures in the foreground, on the left and far right.

He had to paint very quickly to finish them in time for the exhibition opening. See if you can spot them.

The Hay Wain

National Gallery, London, England: www.nationalgallery.org.uk

Critics of Constable's painting style called his white highlights 'Constable's snow'. See what you think of them.

A Burial at Ornans

Musée d'Orsay, Paris, France: www.musee-orsay.fr

If you visit A Burial at Ornans in real life, you will realize how vast it is. It is much longer than most cars!

Ophelia

Tate Britain, London, England: www.tate.org.uk

At Tate Britain, you can also see a larger than life-size sculpture of Millais standing outside the gallery.

La Loge

Courtauld Gallery, Courtauld Institute of Art, London, England: www.courtauld.ac.uk

Textile magnate Samuel Courtauld bought La Loge in 1925, and it now hangs with Paul Cézanne's Mont Sainte-Victoire in the institute Courtauld founded in London in 1932.

Breezing Up (A Fair Wind)

National Gallery of Art, Washington, DC, USA: www.nga.gov

This painting has become one of the best known and most popular images of nineteenth-century American life.

Summer's Day

National Gallery, London, England: www.nationalgallery.org.uk

Berthe Morisot first exhibited this painting in 1880 in the fifth Impressionist exhibition in Paris.

A Sunday on La Grande Jatte

Art Institute of Chicago, Illinois, USA: www.artic.edu

A Sunday on La Grande Jatte is also known as A Sunday Afternoon on the Island of the Grande Jatte.

Mont Sainte-Victoire

Courtauld Gallery, Courtauld Institute of Art, London, England: www.courtauld.ac.uk

Cézanne's work inspired many twentieth-century painters, including Pablo Picasso, and he is often called 'the father of modern art'.

Where Do We Come From? What Are We? Where Are We Going?

Museum of Fine Arts, Boston, Massachusetts, USA: www.mfa.org

If you are interested in Gauguin, you could also try reading Somerset Maugham's 1919 novel The Moon and Sixpence, which was inspired by the artist's life.

Glossary

abstract a work of art that doesn't have a physical subject (such as a person or a landscape) but is concerned with colour, line or tone.

Academician a member of an art academy, usually elected by other members.

altarpiece a painting made to hang above, or stand upon, the altar (communion table) of a church.

bodegone a painting set in a tavern or kitchen, featuring food and drink and sometimes the people who work there.

camera obscura an apparatus that projects images from outside a room on to a wall inside it by means of a lens or mirror.

canvas a cloth stretched over a wooden frame to provide a surface for painting.

cartoon a full-size preparatory drawing for a large artwork that is then used to transfer the design to the final surface.

circa (c.) approximately, as in 'the painting dates from *c.* 1800', i.e. the painting dates from approximately 1800.

classical relating to the ancient Greeks and Romans.

colour wheel in colour theory, a circle showing the relationship between colours.

commission an order for a work of art to be made.

companion piece a work of art designed to be shown alongside another.

complementary colours colours that cause each other to appear brighter when placed next to one another.

composition the arrangement of the parts of a picture.

contrapposto a way of positioning a figure so that the head and shoulders are turned a different way to the hips and legs.

Divisionism, see 'Pointillism'.

Doric a style of classical architecture.

engraver an artist who cuts designs for printing on to metal or wood plates. Ink fills the hollows and can be printed repeatedly on to paper.

Flemish in or from Flanders, a part of Europe now divided between Belgium, France and the Netherlands.

foreground the part of a painted scene that appears nearest the viewer.

fresco a wall-painting made by applying paint on top of wet plaster; when the plaster dries, the painting becomes a permanent part of the wall.

genre scene a type of painting showing adults and children doing everyday activities such as eating or sewing.

gesso a mixture of plaster and glue used to coat wood to create a smooth surface that can be painted on.

glaze a thin, shiny and transparent layer of oil paint.

Grand Tour a tour of Europe, including Italy, to see ancient sculpture, architecture and other cultural sights; in the eighteenth century many young upper-class men took the Grand Tour as part of their education.

ground the surface on which an artist paints.

highlight a bright area in a painting that suggests reflected light.

history painting a painting that tells a story from history, often from ancient Greece or Rome.

Impressionism a painting style adopted by a group of painters who exhibited together eight times in Paris between 1874 and 1886; Impressionists aimed to capture the changeable light and atmosphere as it affected objects, rather than paint in the traditional academic style of the day.

life-size a figure or object painted the size it is in real life.

monochrome a work of art in black and white, or tones of a single colour.

mosaic a type of wall and floor decoration made from small square tiles of glass or stone arranged in patterns; mosaic was used to decorate churches before frescoes and paintings became popular.

Naturalism a style of art based on the accurate depiction of detail.

Neo-Classical an artistic style that copied the art of the ancient Greeks and Romans and influenced painting, sculpture and architecture.

Neo-Impressionism, see 'Pointillism'.

oil paint paint made by mixing powdered colour with an oil such as linseed (flax) oil.

palette a board used to mix paints on.

panel a flat piece of wood used to paint on.

patron someone who supports an artist by commissioning work from them.

perspective a technique that gives paintings the illusion of depth.

pigment a powdered colour used for mixing paint; in the past all colours were made from natural materials, such as stone, metal or even blood, but most modern pigments are synthetic.

plaster a mixture of lime, sand and water used to create a smooth surface on walls: plaster is applied when wet and dries to a flat, hard surface.

Pointillism a painting technique using dots of paint that blend in the viewer's eye to create colours; also known as 'Divisionism' and 'Neo-Impressionism'.

portrait a picture of one or more people.

Pre-Raphaelites a group of nineteenth-century British painters who believed artists should paint directly from nature.

prime to prepare a surface for painting by applying a substance (e.g. gesso) that will help the paint stick.

print an artwork on paper that can be reproduced many times; a design is cut into a metal plate or wooden block, or is drawn on to a stone, then this is inked and pressed on to paper to create an image.

Realism a style of painting in which the artist wants everything they paint to appear lifelike and believable, and not idealized.

relief an artwork that has been carved or modelled so the design stands out from the surface.

Romanticism a style of painting in which an artist's individual emotional response to a subject is valued over academic ability.

Salon an official exhibition of art held at the Louvre in Paris.

scale the relative size of objects when compared to one another.

self-portrait a portrait of the artist painted by him- or herself.

sfumato a painting technique that allows colours to blend into one another, creating a smoky effect.

sitter a person being painted by an artist; someone paid to pose for an artist is called a 'model'.

sketch a drawing in pencil, chalk or sometimes paint; sketches are often produced quickly, and may be used by artists to plan and prepare their artworks.

still life a painted arrangement of inanimate objects such as fruit, flowers, food and kitchenware.

study an artwork done for practice or as an experiment.

symbol an image that represents something else; for example, a dove carrying an olive branch is a symbol of peace.

tempera a type of paint made by mixing powdered colour (pigment) with egg yolk; tempera was widely used before oil paint became popular.

tone the brightness, deepness or intensity of a colour.

watercolour a type of painting, usually on paper, created with fast-drying paints that can be thinned with water to create a translucent effect.

page 55 below *Self-Portrait*, 1806. Pencil on paper, 19 x 14.5 (7$^{1}/_{2}$ x 5$^{11}/_{16}$). Tate, London, England.

Gustave Courbet

page 56 *A Burial at Ornans*, 1850. Oil on canvas, 315 x 668 (124 x 263). Musée d'Orsay, Paris, France.
page 57 *A Burial at Ornans*, 1850 (detail).
page 58 above *Self-Portrait: Man with Pipe*, c. 1848–49. Oil on canvas, 45 x 37 (18$^{1}/_{8}$ x 15). Musée Fabre, Montpellier, France.
page 58 below *After Dinner at Ornans*, 1848–49. Oil on canvas, 195 x 257 (76$^{3}/_{4}$ x 101$^{1}/_{4}$). Palais des Beaux-Arts, Lille, France.
page 59 *The Painter's Studio: A Real Allegory Summing Up Seven Years of My Artistic and Moral Life*, 1855. Oil on canvas, 359 x 598 (141$^{5}/_{16}$ x 235$^{7}/_{16}$). Musée d'Orsay, Paris, France.

John Everett Millais

page 60 *Ophelia*, 1851–52. Oil on canvas, 76.2 x 111.8 (30 x 44). Tate, London, England.
page 61 left *Ophelia*, 1851–52 (detail).
page 61 right *Ophelia*, 1851–52 (detail).
page 62 *Isabella* or *Lorenzo and Isabella*, 1848. Oil on canvas, 101.2 x 140.6 (39$^{13}/_{16}$ x 55$^{3}/_{8}$). Walker Art Gallery, Liverpool, England.
page 63 above *Self-Portrait*, 1883. Oil on canvas, 34.5 x 29.7 (13$^{9}/_{16}$ x 11$^{11}/_{16}$). City of Aberdeen Art Gallery and Museums Collections, Aberdeen, Scotland.
page 63 below *The Boyhood of Raleigh*, 1869–70. Oil on canvas, 120.6 x 142.2 (47$^{1}/_{2}$ x 56). Tate, London, England.

Pierre-Auguste Renoir

page 64 *La Loge*, 1874. Oil on canvas, 80 x 63.5 (31$^{1}/_{2}$ x 25). Courtauld Gallery, Courtauld Institute of Art, London, England.
page 65 left *La Loge*, 1874 (detail).
page 65 right *La Loge*, 1874 (detail).
page 66 above *Self-Portrait*, c. 1875. Oil on canvas, 39.4 x 31.8 (15$^{1}/_{2}$ x 12$^{1}/_{2}$). Sterling and Francine Clark Art Institute, Williamstown, Massachusetts, USA.
page 66 below *The Luncheon of the Boating Party*, 1880–81. Oil on canvas, 130 x 175.5 (51$^{1}/_{4}$ x 69). Phillips Collection, Washington, DC, USA.

page 67 *The Umbrellas*, c. 1881–86. Oil on canvas, 180.3 x 114.9 (71 x 45$^{1}/_{4}$). National Gallery, London, England.

Winslow Homer

page 68 *Breezing Up (A Fair Wind)*, 1876. Oil on canvas, 61.5 x 97 (24$^{1}/_{8}$ x 38$^{1}/_{8}$). National Gallery of Art, Washington, DC, USA, Gift of the W. L. and May T. Mellon Foundation, 1943.13.1.
page 69 left *Breezing Up (A Fair Wind)*, 1876 (detail).
page 69 right *Breezing Up (A Fair Wind)*, 1876 (detail).
page 70 above Napoleon Sarony, *Portrait of Winslow Homer*, 1880. Photograph. Bowdoin College Museum of Art, Brunswick, Maine, USA, 1964.69.179.4, Gift of the Homer Family.
page 70 below *Boy Fishing*, 1892. Watercolour on paper, 37.2 x 71.1 (14$^{5}/_{8}$ x 28). San Antonio Museum of Art, Texas, USA.
page 71 *Home, Sweet Home*, 1863. Oil on canvas, 54.6 x 41.9 (21$^{1}/_{2}$ x 16$^{1}/_{2}$). Private Collection.

Berthe Morisot

page 72 *Summer's Day*, 1879. Oil on canvas, 45.7 x 75.2 (18 x 29$^{5}/_{8}$). National Gallery, London, England.
page 73 *Summer's Day*, 1879 (detail).
page 74 left Édouard Manet, *Berthe Morisot with a Bouquet of Violets*, 1872. Oil on canvas, 55 x 38 (21$^{5}/_{8}$ x 15). Musée d'Orsay, Paris, France.
page 74 right *Jeune Femme en Toilette de Bal (Young Woman Dressed for the Ball)*, 1879. Oil on canvas, 71 x 54 (28 x 21$^{1}/_{4}$). Musée d'Orsay, Paris, France.
page 75 *Eugène Manet and his Daughter in the Garden at Bougival*, 1881. Oil on canvas, 73 x 92 (28$^{3}/_{4}$ x 36$^{1}/_{4}$). Musée Marmottan, Paris, France. Foundation Denis and Annie Rouart.

Georges Seurat

page 76 *A Sunday on La Grande Jatte*, 1884–86. Oil on canvas, 205.7 x 308.1 (81$^{3}/_{4}$ x 121$^{1}/_{4}$). Art Institute of Chicago, Illinois, USA. Helen Birch Bartlett Memorial Collection, 1926.224.
page 77 left *A Sunday on La Grande Jatte*, 1884–86 (detail).
page 77 right *A Sunday on La Grande Jatte*, 1884–86 (detail).
page 78 above Photograph of Georges Seurat by unknown photographer.

page 78 below *Bathers at Asnières*, 1884. Oil on canvas, 201 x 300 (79$^{1}/_{8}$ x 118$^{1}/_{8}$). National Gallery, London, England.
page 79 *The Circus*, 1891. Oil on canvas, 185.5 x 152.5 (73$^{1}/_{16}$ x 60$^{1}/_{16}$). Musée d'Orsay, Paris, France.

Paul Cézanne

page 80 *Mont Sainte-Victoire*, 1887. Oil on canvas, 66.8 x 92.3 (26$^{5}/_{16}$ x 36$^{5}/_{16}$). Courtauld Gallery, Courtauld Institute of Art, London, England.
page 81 left *Mont Sainte-Victoire*, 1887 (detail).
page 81 right *Mont Sainte-Victoire*, 1887 (detail).
page 82 above *Mont Sainte-Victoire*, 1900–02. Watercolour, 31 x 48 (12$^{3}/_{16}$ x 18$^{7}/_{8}$). Cabinet des Dessins, Musée du Louvre, Paris, France.
page 82 below *Self-Portrait*, 1880–81. Oil on canvas, 34.7 x 27 (13$^{11}/_{16}$ x 10$^{5}/_{8}$). National Gallery, London, England.
page 83 *Still Life with a Plaster Cast*, 1894. Oil on prepared paper mounted on panel, 70.6 x 57.3 (27$^{13}/_{16}$ x 22$^{9}/_{16}$). Courtauld Gallery, Courtauld Institute of Art, London, England.

Paul Gauguin

page 84 *Where Do We Come From? What Are We? Where Are We Going?*, 1897–98. Oil on canvas, 139.1 x 374.6 (54$^{3}/_{4}$ x 147$^{1}/_{2}$). Museum of Fine Arts Boston, Massachusetts, USA, Tompkins Collection, Arthur Gordon Tompkins Fund, 1936, 36.270.
page 85 left *Where Do We Come From? What Are We? Where Are We Going?*, 1897–98 (detail).
page 85 right *Where Do We Come From? What Are We? Where Are We Going?*, 1897–98 (detail).
page 86 left *Self-Portrait*, 1889. Oil on wood, 79.2 x 51.3 (31$^{3}/_{16}$ x 20$^{3}/_{16}$). National Gallery of Art, Washington, DC, USA.
page 86 right *The Vision After the Sermon*, 1888. Oil on canvas, 73 x 92 (28$^{3}/_{4}$ x 36$^{1}/_{4}$). National Gallery of Scotland, Edinburgh, Scotland.
page 87 *Women of Tahiti* or *On the Beach*, 1891. Oil on canvas, 69 x 91.5 (27$^{1}/_{8}$ x 36). Musée d'Orsay, Paris, France.

About The Author

Charlie Ayres studied at the Courtauld Institute of Art and Sotheby's Institute in London. Under the name Charlotte Mullins, she edited *Art Review* and *V&A Magazine*. She has written widely on art, and her previous children's publications include *Lives of the Great Artists*. She lives in London with her husband and two children.

First published in 2010 in hardcover in the United States of America by Thames & Hudson Inc., 500 Fifth Avenue, New York, New York 10110

thamesandhudsonusa.com

Library of Congress Catalog Card Number 2010923293

ISBN 978-0-500-23880-6

Printed and bound in China by Toppan Printing

DATE DUE

GAYLORD | PRINTED IN U.S.A.